SABINE LIPPERT'S
BEADED FANTASIES

SABINE LIPPERT'S
BEADED FANTASIES

30 Romantic Jewelry Projects

LARK CRAFTS

Asheville

Editor
Nathalie Mornu

Technical Editor
Judith Durant

Art Director
Kathleen Holmes

Junior Designer
Carol Morse Barnao

Layout
Jackie Kerr

Illustrator
J'aime Allene

Photographer
Lynne Harty

Cover Designer
Kathleen Holmes

Editorial Assistance
Dawn Dillingham, Abby Haffelt

Editorial Intern
Katherine Clark

LARK CRAFTS

An Imprint of Sterling Publishing
387 Park Avenue South
New York, NY 10016

If you have questions or comments about
this book, please visit: larkcrafts.com

Library of Congress Cataloging-in-Publication Data

Lippert, Sabine, 1967-
  Sabine Lippert's beaded fantasies : 30 romantic jewelry projects / Sabine Lippert. -- 1st ed.
    p. cm. -- (Beadweaving master class series)
  ISBN 978-1-4547-0246-7 (hardback)
  1. Beadwork--Patterns. 2. Jewelry making. I. Title.
  TT860.L49 2012
  746.5--dc23

                                   2011037349

10 9 8 7 6 5 4 3 2 1

First Edition

Published by Lark Crafts
An Imprint of Sterling Publishing Co., Inc.
387 Park Avenue South, New York, NY 10016

Text © 2012, Sabine Lippert
Photography © 2012, Lark Crafts, an Imprint of Sterling Publishing Co., Inc., unless otherwise specified
Photos on pages 81, 91, 92 and 125 - 130 © 2012 Sabine Lippert
Illustrations © 2012, Lark Crafts, an Imprint of Sterling Publishing Co., Inc., unless otherwise specified

Distributed in Canada by Sterling Publishing,
c/o Canadian Manda Group, 165 Dufferin Street, Toronto, Ontario, Canada M6K 3H6

Distributed in the United Kingdom by GMC Distribution Services,
Castle Place, 166 High Street, Lewes, East Sussex, England BN7 1XU

Distributed in Australia by Capricorn Link (Australia) Pty Ltd.,
P.O. Box 704, Windsor, NSW 2756 Australia

Manufactured in China

ISBN 13: 978-1-4547-0246-7

For information about custom editions, special sales, and premium and corporate
purchases, please contact the Sterling Special Sales Department at 800-805-5489 or
specialsales@sterlingpub.com.

Requests for information about desk and examination copies available to college and university
professors must be submitted to academic@larkbooks.com. Our complete policy can be found at
www.larkcrafts.com.

56

51

24

69

74

100

85

96

40

48

21

111

60

66

18

CONTENTS

26

6

121

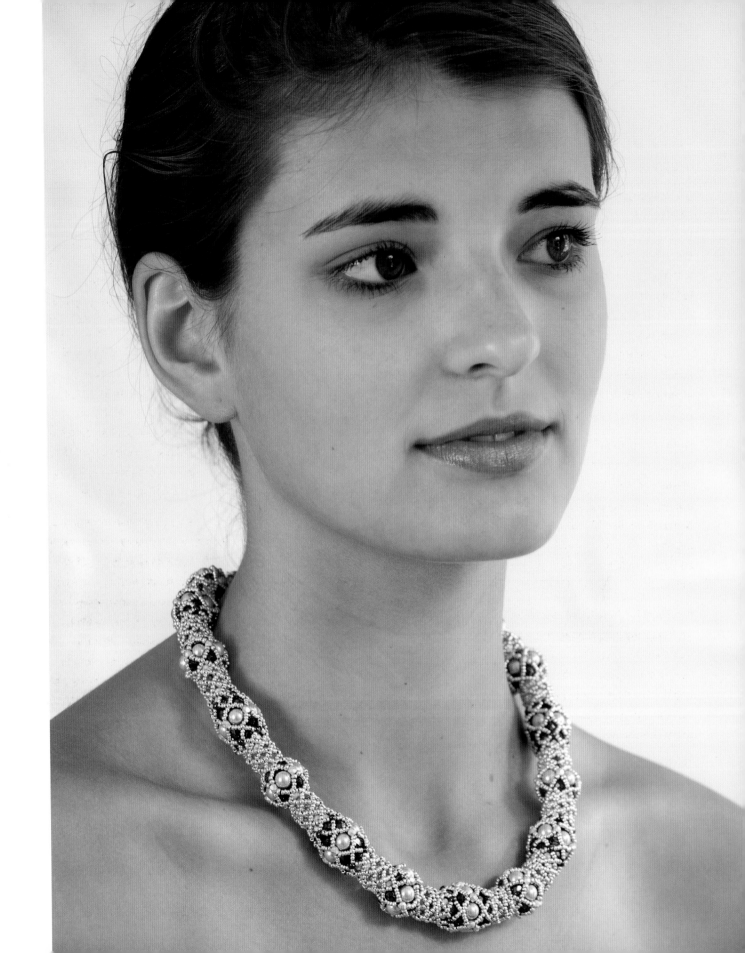

INTRODUCTION

I WANT TO "INFECT" YOU WITH

MY OBSESSION WITH BEADS.

By profession, I'm a medical doctor. You might think that beads would be a welcome change to the daily routine, but crafting was my passion long before my career started. When I was a child, my mother always insisted on crafting with me and my sister—drawing, crochet, cross stitch, knitting. (Mom still has my kindergarden paintings and she continues to wear my first attempts at beading. I've tried to convince her to put on only my latest designs, but she's a bit more stubborn than I am.) My father, an engineer, introduced me to woodworking, tinkering with minor electrical repairs around the house, and ruining the family's pots and pans while making candy.

From the moment I first touched beads, I became totally addicted. The multitude of shapes, colors, and materials still mesmerizes me. My friends have embraced the fact that I always bring along my beads when we get together; they know I'm unbearable without them. I bead on airplanes. I bead on weekends. I bead before work, on my lunch break, and all evening long. Rumor has it I even bead while I'm asleep, but there's no solid evidence of that … yet.

Beadwork is where technical skill intersects with the arts. And since my parents long ago convinced me I could fearlessly take a crack at anything (except for fixing TVs—they can burn down the house if you fix them wrong, and that's a direct quote from my Dad), my ever-growing collection of pearls, crystals, chatons, and rivolis invites me to try one beaded experiment after another.

The instructions in this book represent some of my best designs, from necklaces and pendants to earrings and bracelets. I start off with a section of basic information, including how to execute my favorite stitches, right angle weave and peyote. The 30 projects include Milady Pendant (page 77), a sparkling pendant of golden rivolis and large deep-green pearls that looks straight out of a Baroque painting. For the hefty Purple Rope Necklace (page 111), a netting of silver seed beads enfolds pale violet pearls and eggplant-colored beads. Golden charms hanging from the oval beaded bead of the Aisha Earrings (page 94) lend these dangles an oriental look. And my La Fleur Bracelet (page 45) features a narrow strip of delicate flowers beaded in bronze with chaton centers in a milky turquoise; this confection would have caused Marie Antoinette to swoon with delight.

I end with a chapter that describes my approach to design, including tips on how I alter the construction methods of a piece to allow it to evolve in directions that sometimes look radically different from the original intention. I hope this section encourages you, too, to branch out in your beadwork and gives you concrete suggestions for doing so. Finally, in the last few pages, you'll find gallery images of my own work, as well as that of some of the beaders I most admire. May these photos inspire you to strive further!

People sometimes ask me if I ever fail while making a project. Yes, I do, a thousand times, but failure is always something to learn from, both for me and for you. Be brave and confident. Use this book as a starting point, then try your own designs. I had a violin teacher long ago who would throw up her hands: "You're not playing what the composer wrote!" My answer, already back then, was, "So what? It sounds good, doesn't it?" Make my designs with this same attitude. Subsitute one note—or bead—for another, add a trill here or there. Though a project may start with a specific idea, midway through, the beads can lead you somewhere completely different. It's fine, let it grow. Something much better might come of it. Just listen to the sound of your beads.

Sabine
Lippert

CHAPTER 1
SUPPLIES AND TECHNIQUES

There are thousands of beads to choose from and countless ways to put them together to make jewelry. Here, I describe the beads, tools, and methods I use for my creations.

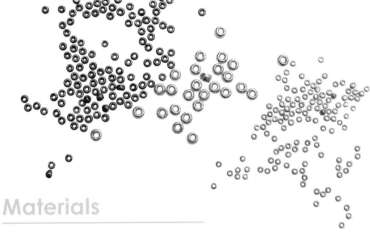

Materials

Beads come in so many different shapes, sizes, colors, and coatings that it's not easy to give a complete overview. Instead, I'll tell you a little about the beads I like best, and why I prefer them.

▶ Seed Beads

If a piece of beadwork requires a uniform size of seed beads, I choose Japanese beads. I use different sizes, usually 15°, 11°, 8°, and sometimes 6°. (The smaller the number, by the way, the larger the bead.) They also come in two shapes: round beads (called seed beads in this book) and cylinder beads (also known as Delica beads). While cylinder beads are perfect for peyote stitch techniques, especially when you want to create a stiff, stable piece, seed beads are ideal for right angle weave and netting.

▶ Drop Beads and Magatamas

These beads, also known as fringe beads, are perfect for emphasizing special areas of your beadwork. Because their holes face sideways, when added to beadwork, these types of beads will lie on the surface of the beading. I use drop beads to highlight netting structures or to embellish right angle weave. Magatamas are a bit flatter than drop beads and have a bigger hole.

▶ Fire-Polished Beads

These have a shape somewhere between a round bead and a bicone bead. They're perfect for building bases in right angle weave or cubic right angle weave, and I love the millions of colors and finishes they come in. They're not quite as flashy as crystals, but they do have a wonderful shine.

▶ Bicone Crystals

I prefer Austrian crystals, especially for their brilliant colors and perfect cut. The new generation of beads is being manufactured with softened edges, so broken jewelry caused by frayed threads is becoming rare. Bicone beads add beautiful highlights to any piece of beadwork.

▶ Round Beads

I use both crystal and synthetic glass pearls. In either case, high quality is preferred. Most especially, the coating should not be too thin. To assess their quality, handle the beads—the heavier they are, the better.

▶ Focal Beads, Fancy Stones, and Rivolis

These beads are the grail of bead hunters and collectors. Some sizes are available in a large range of colors and coatings, while other sizes are hard to find. Because of this I always recommend that if you come across it and like it, buy it! Sooner or later you'll discover the perfect project for which to use it.

Colors and Coatings

Opaque beads have the most stable color, but if you want more glamorous or fancy effects, you need beads with other finishes or coatings. Galvanized beads come in beautiful metallic colors, but some of them begin to lose their surface during the beading process and it gets worse over time. There are new finishes available—for example, Duracoat, by Miyuki, and Toho's PF (permanent finish) beads—that are much more stable, but you still have to remember that a coating is a coating and it can rub off. Keep this in mind while planning a piece; for areas that will have direct contact with skin, you should choose a more stable finish.

▶ Clasps

You could write an entire book about clasps—every beader prefers something different. You can make beaded clasps such as toggles or loops slung around a button, and there are sliders, magnetic clasps, and hooks. Commercial clasps are made of different materials, some cheap, others more expensive, and the range of possibilities is wide.

The cheapest clasp is one you bead yourself, but because the clasp is the most used part of the beadwork, beaded toggles can lose their beauty after a short time. Remember, the coating on beads will rub off from skin contact.

When I first started beading, I bought a lot of cheap clasps, which I regretted later on. They broke easily, lost their coatings, or oxidized. After spending endless hours of valuable time beading with high-quality beads and creating a beautiful piece of jewelry, you don't want to destroy it all by skimping on the quality of the clasp.

▶ Thread

I've tried a lot of different threads and from talking with other people, it's clear that each beader has his or her own preference.

Most of the time I use FireLine, especially in the smoke color. It's a non-elastic, multifilament, braided thread that's covered

with a protective surface. You should not make knots in this thread; they destroy the surface and therefore the stability. Smoke FireLine is more subtle than crystal Fire-Line—it almost disappears into the beadwork. The thread is sometimes a bit stiff, but you can soften it with a thread conditioner.

I use two kinds of multifilament nylon threads: One G from Toho and KO thread from Miyuki. They're preconditioned so, unlike with other nylon threads, you don't need to use a thread conditioner. They're a bit elastic and perfect for beadwork where you need to keep good tension on the thread.

Length of Thread

People often ask me why in my beading instructions I don't say anything about the required length of thread. The answer is very easy: The length should be comfortable for you; when you run out of thread, start a new one. I always use a wingspan of thread, no more. If your thread is too long, you'll waste a lot of time untangling it; if it's too short, you'll have difficulty maintaining tension in your beadwork.

If your thread starts to tangle, get frizzy, or split, start a new one. The quality of the thread is of major importance to the stability and endurance of the finished piece. Sometimes I see students struggling for a long time with a short, destroyed piece of thread. Just cutting a new one can save a lot of time!

Knots

There's a running joke in the workshops I teach. If someone asks, "Don't we make a knot in the beginning?" the students who already know me always chime in when I answer, "In my classes you can do whatever you like, but not a knot!"

I nearly never make knots in my beadwork. I also never use stopper beads. (A stopper bead is one used temporarily at the end of the thread—it's held on by a loop—to prevent the other beads from slipping off. When I've used stopper beads, I've had problems with maintaining thread tension; if the stopper is attached too well, you can't remove it easily later on, but if you don't fasten it properly, the stopper will slide along the thread.) When starting a project, I hold the thread tail slung around my left hand, string the required beads, and then form them into a ring or whatever's needed. I don't let go of the tail until the beads are secured, which usually happens after the second or third row. I do this for several reasons:

- Holding the tail in one hand and the needle in the other allows you to work with good tension. When I've made knots to close a loop of beads that are the

starting row of a piece, I've always have the feeling that the loop is either too tight or too loose.

- A knot can obstruct your bead hole, and it can shred your thread and make it unstable.

- Weaving two or three times through the beads of the first step secures the thread so you can cut the tail off later on.

▶ Thread Conditioners

Thread Heaven is a conditioner that makes your thread less stiff and helps it slip much more easily through beads. I've tried beading wax, but it's too sticky for me. It's good, however, if you have difficulties keeping tension on your thread, or if you want to work with a doubled thread.

Tools

You don't need too many tools for the projects in this book.

Beading Needles

I do nearly all my beadwork with size 12 beading needles. Keep one size 13 needle for backup; you might need it near the end of a project because the holes of the beads are packed with thread, preventing a larger needle from passing through, or when you're using very small beads, like size 15° Czech beads or other beads with tiny holes.

▶ Scissors

Scissors should be fine but strong and sharp. I prefer cutting my thread with scissors, but I also have a thread burner that I use when there are very short tails of thread. Some beaders prefer to cut FireLine with dedicated scissors, because it can dull the blades. I always tend to forget to use a dedicated tool, and my scissors hold up well without damage.

▶ Pliers

I use three kinds of pliers: round-nose pliers to bend loops, two pairs of flat-nose pliers with a narrow tip to open jump rings, and cutters to shorten a wire or head pin. The higher the quality of the pliers, the longer they'll last.

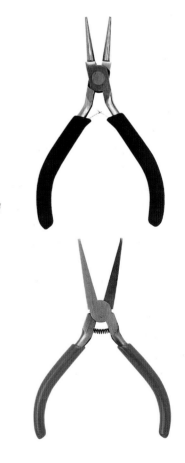

Basic Techniques

As previously mentioned, there are many methods that can be used to join beads together. Here are the techniques used for the projects in this book.

▶ Peyote Stitch

The most common peyote stitch is one-drop. You pick up a line of beads for the first row, and in the second row you add one bead, skip one bead, and pass through the next bead. Repeat this until you reach the end of the row, at which point you change direction and continue as described for the next row, adding one bead, skipping one bead, and passing through the next bead (figure 1).

Circular peyote uses the same technique, but you start with a line of beads that you close into a ring. Pick up one bead, skip one bead, and pass through the next bead. When you finish the ring, you have to step up, which means you pass again through the first bead you added in this row. From there, you start the next row (figure 2).

I rarely use one-drop peyote in my beadwork, usually adding a mix of one, two, three, or more beads in one step. The different bead counts make increasing or decreasing the circumference very easy. Figure 3 shows how you can easily vary the bead count in a peyote pattern.

figure 1

figure 2

figure 3

▶ Right Angle Weave

Right angle weave, abbreviated as RAW throughout this book, is the most versatile stitch and the base of many of my beading projects. It's so named because of the thread path through the beads.

1 Pick up four beads and go through the first one to form a ring. The thread path now looks square, and between the beads, it changes direction at a right angle.

2 Pick up three more beads, build a loop around the bead from which the thread exited, and weave again through this bead. Then weave through the beads so the thread exits the second bead added in this step.

3 Add another three beads. As you can see in figure 4, the direction will alternate between clockwise and counterclockwise.

When you add the second row, continue with this stitch, but include the beads of the previous row. After building several rows, you can see "crossing points" between the beads, which are represented by red dots in figure 5. Never weave straight through these crossing points, or your thread will show.

Tip: Some beaders have difficulties with this stitch, mainly because they lose their way through the beadwork. This often happens when they pull the thread through the piece and let it slip out of their fingers. I tell my students to hold the piece down on the beading mat with one hand. Then the piece stays in the same position and you don't lose your point of reference. Because of their size and shape, fire-polished beads are perfect for taking your first steps with this stitch.

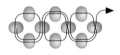

figure 4

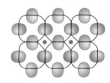

figure 5

▶ Cubic Right Angle Weave

Regular RAW units are squares with four sides. With six squares, you can build a cube, and that's exactly what you do with cubic RAW. Many roads lead to Rome, and many ways lead to this technique. To better orient myself, I try to imagine that the cube is a little room—it has a floor, four side walls, and a ceiling.

1 Start by making the floor: Pick up four beads and build a square (figure 6).

2 Pick up another three beads and weave through the bead from which the thread exited, and then forward through the last bead in the floor (figure 7).

3 Flip up the beads added in step 2, your first wall. Pick up two new beads, weave through the bead of the previous wall and the bead of the floor from which the thread exited, then forward through the next bead of the floor (figure 8). This is the back wall.

4 Repeat step 3 to build the third wall. At the end, weave forward through the bead of the floor and the bead of the first wall (figure 9).

5 To build the fourth wall, pick up one bead and weave through all four beads of this wall, as shown in figure 10.

6 Now the cube (or room) is nearly finished. With all four walls up, weave through the four beads at the top of the walls to close up the ceiling (figure 11).

In this illustration, the room made in cubic RAW is shown from above.

Beads 1, 2, 3, and 4 make up the floor. Beads 5, 6, 7, and 2 are the first wall. The second wall consists of beads 8, 9, 5, and 3. The third wall is made from beads 10, 11, 8, and 4. Beads 10, 12, 7, and 1 are the final wall. To tighten the ceiling, weave through beads 12, 11, 9, and 6. The ceiling of the first unit will become the floor of the next unit.

You can also attach the cubes in the second row—imagine that you include the walls of the adjacent units in the ones you already constructed.

▶ Tubular Right Angle Weave

Tubular RAW can be made in two different ways. One way is to bead a flat piece of RAW and, once it's finished, roll it into a tube held together with a zipping row, joining the first row to the last. When you bring these rows together, the left and the right beads of the RAW unit already exist; you add just one bead to the bottom of the first unit and one bead to the top. To continue zipping the rows together, you need only add one bead to the top of each subsequent unit.

In some of my beaded beads, you'll find the other version of this technique, which is more related to cubic RAW except that you start with a larger (or smaller) number of beads for the "floor." For example, you start with six beads that are connected into a ring; those are the floor. Then you bead six walls—add three beads for the first wall, two beads for the second through fifth walls, and then one bead for the sixth wall. Finally, you weave once in a circle through the six beads of the ceiling. The thread path is the same as for cubic RAW.

figure 6

figure 7

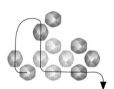

figure 8

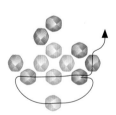

figure 9

figure 10

figure 11

▶ Fringe and Picots

I try to avoid having any visible thread in my pieces, so I add fringe or picots to cover sides of the beadwork where thread shows. A picot is the smallest fringe you can make; you exit a bead, pick up three beads, and pass back through the same bead the thread exited or the adjacent bead. Fringes can be made in endless variations. What they all have in common is that you string a number of beads, add one or several beads to create the end of the fringe, than weave back through the strung beads. If you only use one bead at the end of a fringe, the thread might show, so I prefer to have at least three small beads at the tip, building a little picot.

▶ Loops

I use loops to attach jump rings or clasps. I usually make them from size 11° or 15° seed beads, or a combination of the two.

1 With the thread exiting the bead where you want to add the loop (shown in a contrasting color in figure 12) string five or seven size 11° seed beads, pass again through the bead the thread exited, and then weave at least twice through all the beads of the loop to add strength.

2 To make the loop really stiff, which is important for its stability, add one size 15° seed bead in the four gaps between the 11° beads in the loop (figure 13).

figure 12

figure 13

▶ Attaching Clasps

After experiencing difficulties with broken clasps in the past, I've made a few observations.

Magnetic clasps should not be attached in a stiff way. The effect of leverage can make the clasps disconnect, even if the clasp itself is strong. If you attach the clasps by using jump rings as links, this won't happen, and the jewelry will stay on.

A clasp must be easy to remove without destroying the beaded piece. This is why I try to avoid sewing clasps to a piece. Instead, I make a loop of beads and mount the clasp to this loop with a jump ring. If the clasp is ever damaged, you can replace it with a new clasp simply by opening the jump ring. If you must sew on the clasp, use a separate thread—if you have to remove it, you won't destroy your beadwork.

▶ Bending a Head Pin

There are different ways to form the loop on a head pin. The method to choose depends on the material the head pin is made from. If you have a strong material, you can cut the head pin about ⅜ inch (1 cm) above the bead, bend it to one side at a 90° angle, then use round-nose pliers to form a loop. If you have a softer material, like silver wire, leave a longer end, bend it at a 90° angle, and then roll it twice to form a double loop.

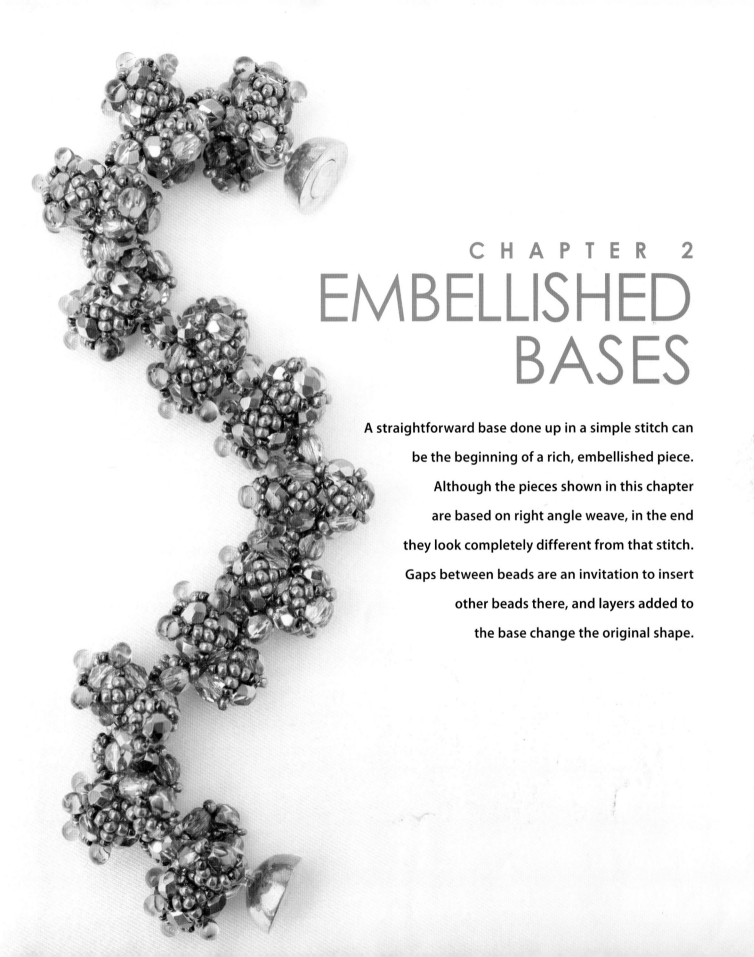

CHAPTER 2

EMBELLISHED BASES

A straightforward base done up in a simple stitch can be the beginning of a rich, embellished piece. Although the pieces shown in this chapter are based on right angle weave, in the end they look completely different from that stitch. Gaps between beads are an invitation to insert other beads there, and layers added to the base change the original shape.

ART DECO NECKLACE

At first sight, this necklace might look complicated, but it's nothing more than a line of embellished right angle weave. The different sizes of beads create the elegant shape.

1 Using 15° seed beads, make a strip of four units in RAW. This is the strip that will attach to the clasp, and you can add units to adjust the necklace length as needed before adding the clasp. For the next unit, string one 15°, one 11°, and one 15°; end exiting the 11° seed bead. For the next unit add three 11°s. For the following unit string two 11°s, one 4-mm pearl, and two 11°s—each pair of 11°s counts as one bead in this unit. The next unit requires two 4-mm pearls and one 3-mm bicone. This unit is the center of the sequence. For the next unit string five 11°s (the two pairs again count as one bead each in the unit). Add one unit with three 11°s, one unit with three 15°s, and one unit with two 15°s and one 11°. This is the middle unit between the sequences (figure 1).

2 Continue beading these sequences until the necklace reaches the desired length (the necklace pictured here shows 15 sequences). At the end, bead a strip of RAW units with 15°s as you did at the start, adjusting the number of units on both ends if necessary to achieve the desired necklace length.

3 In the following two steps you'll bead along the exterior of this band of RAW units. Refer to figure 2 (next page). The side with the bicones is the outer edge of the necklace, and you'll start along the inner edge, starting with the RAW units of 15° at the beginning. With the thread exiting the 15° bead at the inner edge of the first RAW unit, pick up one 15° and pass through the corresponding 15° in the next unit; repeat until you've added one 15° to each of these units. Then, between the 15° just exited and the next 11°, add two 15°s; weave through the next three 11°s (you skip one gap without adding a bead here!), add two 15°s, and pass through the next pearl. String six 15°s and build an arc above the pearl by passing through the pearl again.

String two 15°s and weave through the next three 11°s. String two 15°s, pass through the next 15°, then add one 15° in each of the following two gaps. This completes one sequence. Beginning with two 15°s in front of the next size 11° seed bead, repeat the pattern along the whole inner edge of the necklace.

figure 1

SUPPLIES

Size 15° galvanized gold
seed beads, 4 g

Size 11° matte metallic
gray seed beads, 4 g

45 antique brass pearls, 4 mm

15 olive-green AB crystal
bicones, 3 mm

44 size 8° bronze seed beads

14 antique brass drop pearls,
8 x 11 mm

14 olive-green with bronze effect
crystal bicones, 4 mm

2 golden jump rings

1 golden clasp

FireLine, smoke, 6-pound test

Size 12 beading needle

Small sharp scissors

FINISHED SIZE

16 inches (40.5 cm),
not including clasp

At the outer edge of the necklace, add one 15° to the RAW units of 15°s as was done for the inner edge. With the thread exiting the last 15° in this strip, pick up one size 8° seed bead and pass through the first 11° on the outside edge; pick up one 15° and weave through the next two 11°s; string two 11°s and pass through the 3-mm bicone. Repeat the steps in reverse until you reach the 11° bead in the middle, between two sequences, and add two 15°s before and after this bead. Repeat this pattern along the whole outer edge of the necklace.

4 Begin again at the inner edge and weave through the beadwork to add one 15° to the middle of each arc above the pearls. It's important to add these beads in this second step, or the arcs will flip to the front or back of the necklace.

Weave along the outer edge and add three 15°s above the 3-mm bicone beads, and a fringe with the drop beads between size 8° beads, as follows. With the thread exiting a size 8° bead, string four 15°s, one 8°, one drop, one 4-mm bicone, and three 15°s. Pass back through the bicone, the drop, and the 8°. String four 15°s and pass through the next 8°. Repeat the pattern along the whole outer edge of the necklace (figure 3).

5 At the beginning and the end, make a loop of seven 15° seed beads; attach the clasp to these loops with jump rings.

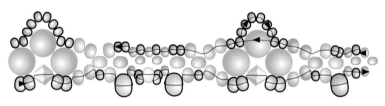

figure 2

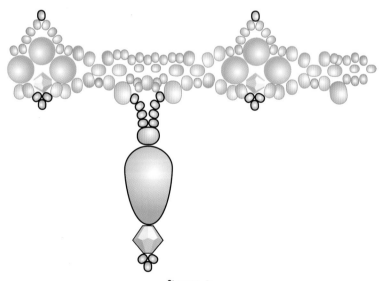

figure 3

CUBIC DOTS BRACELET

This bracelet is a mix of flat RAW and cubic RAW, embellished with seed beads and drop beads. I've already found so many possible variations on rich embellished RAW bases made from fire-polished beads, and I know I'll discover still more.

SUPPLIES

240 marigold coated fire-polished beads, 4 mm

Size 15° dark bronze seed beads, 3 g

Size 11° galvanized reddish brown seed beads, 5 g

60 crystal pink-lined drop beads, 3.4 mm

2 golden jump rings

1 golden magnetic clasp

FireLine, 6-pound test

Size 12 beading needle

Small sharp scissors

2 pairs of flat-nose pliers

FINISHED SIZE

7¾ inches (19.7 cm), not including clasp

2 The surface of the component you just made is made up of five RAW units: one lies flat next to the basic ring, one is vertical (climbing up), one is flat (on top of the cube, opposite the basic ring), one is vertical (climbing down), and one lies flat on the other side of the basic ring. (Figure 2 shows the units as they would appear in a flat row.) Along these units, you'll weave the first layer of embellishment with cross-stitches. With the thread exiting the first fire-polished bead at the beginning of the component, string one size 15°, three 11°s, and one 15°; cross the first RAW unit and pass through the next fire-polished bead. Repeat this step for the next RAW unit (climbing-up unit).

For the top unit, pick up one 15°, one 11°, one drop bead, one 11°, and one 15°. Cover the next two units in the same way as the first two. At the end, string one 15° and one 11°, pass through the middle of the three 11°s, add one 11° and one 15°, and pass through the next fire-polished bead. Continue in this fashion to complete cross-stitches on all five units.

Note: There are two possible ways to bead this bracelet. You can first create the entire base, then embellish it in a second step, or you can make it unit by unit, embellishing each one as you finish it. I prefer the second option, because I love to see the piece take shape little by little. So those are the instructions I give you here.

1 Build one cube in RAW using the fire-polished beads, as follows. String four beads and pass through the first bead strung to create a ring (this is the basic ring). Weave through the beads again. String three beads and weave through the bead from which the thread exited and through the next bead in the basic ring. The new unit of four beads is the first side unit.

String two beads and weave through the bead in the previous side unit and the bead from which the thread exited (second side unit). Pass through the next bead in the basic ring, string two beads, and weave through the bead in the previous side unit and the bead from which the thread exited (third side unit). Now

weave forward through the next bead in the basic ring and the bead in the first side unit. Pick up one new bead and weave through the bead in the previous side unit, the base, and the bead from which the thread exited. Weave in a circle through the four beads opposite the basic ring.

The cube is now finished. Build one RAW unit on the left and one on the right side of the cube, starting from the beads in the basic ring. Figure 1 shows the unit from the side and from the top.

Side view   Top view

figure 1

3 The base of the component consists of three RAW units. Weave along the outside of these three units and add one 11° seed bead after each fire-polished bead (eight 11°s total). Then weave up to the RAW unit on top and weave around the four fire-polished beads in the top unit, adding one drop bead in each corner. Figure 3 shows the unit from the side.

4 After finishing this first component, you'll build a link to the next unit. Add one RAW unit made of fire-polished beads at the center of the base (outlined in green in figure 3) and cover this unit with cross-stitches as before (one 15°, three 11°, and one 15°, then one 15°, one 11°, pass through the middle 11°, and add one 11° and one 15°).

5 On the other end of this link, make a RAW unit of fire-polished beads. This unit is the basic ring of the next cubic RAW component. Repeat all steps to build a rope of 12 components connected by 11 links. Weave through the end components several times to strengthen them.

6 Attach the clasp to the basic rings on each end of the rope with jump rings.

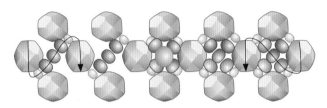

figure 2

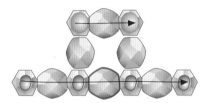

figure 3

24

SUPPLIES

26 copper fire-polished beads, 4 mm

6 purple satin round beads, 6 mm

Size 11° galvanized rose seed beads, <1 g

12 violet gold-luster drop beads, 3.4 mm

Size 15° light gold seed beads, <1 g

12 pale matte rose 2XAB crystal bicones, 3 mm

6 mauve glass pearls, 4 mm

2 copper head pins with decorative small metal head

2 copper ear wires

FireLine, 6-pound test

Size 12 beading needle

Round-nose pliers

Flat-nose pliers

FINISHED SIZE

¾ inch (1.9 cm) tall, not including ear wires

LITTLE LANTERN EARRINGS

This design is a variation on my Scheherezade patterns in chapter 4, but based on a triangular shape. Combining different bead sizes and shapes, these delicate earrings are easy to make and offer endless possibilities.

1 Make the first RAW unit as follows: String three fire-polished beads, then go through the first bead strung to form a ring. Weave three times through all the beads. This is the basic ring.

2 Continue with RAW units as follows: String one fire-polished bead, one 6-mm round, and one fire-polished bead; pass again through the bead from which the thread originally exited. Pass through the next bead in the basic ring. String one fire-polished bead and one 6-mm round, and

weave through the fire-polished bead in the previous RAW unit, then the fire-polished bead from which the thread exited. Weave forward through the third bead in the basic ring and the fire-polished bead in the first RAW unit; pick up one 6-mm round and weave again through the four beads in this last RAW unit. Weave twice through the three 6-mm round beads (figure 1).

Starting from one 6-mm round bead, build three RAW units on the other side of the 6-mm beads, using fire-polished beads only, then weave twice through the center three fire-polished beads in each unit to form a ring like the original basic ring.

3 With the thread exiting a fire-polished bead on the top ring, string one 11°, one drop, and one 11°, and pass through the next fire-polished bead—one drop picot made. Repeat two more times, then weave to the other side and add three drop picots to the original basic ring. End with the thread exiting a size 11° seed bead in front of a fire-polished bead (figure 2).

4 You'll add the netting in this step. The beads of the first part are outlined in red in figure 3. String two 15°s, one bicone, and two 15°s, and pass through the next drop picot. Repeat two more times. End with the thread exiting a bicone.

The beads in the next part are outlined in green in figure 3. String one 11° and two 15°s, then pass through the 6-mm round (the bead below the bicone). String two 15°s and one 11°, and pass again through the bicone, forming netting between the 6-mm bead and the bicone. Weave forward so the thread exits the same 6-mm round. String two 15°s, one 11°, one bicone, one 11°, and two 15°s; pass again through the 6-mm round, forming an arc. Weave forward through the next 6-mm round and repeat the two parts of the netting here (meaning the connection to the bicone of the previous step on one side and an arc on the other side). Repeat once more with the third 6-mm round. Weave forward to exit the bicone in an arc added in this step.

The beads in this part are outlined in purple. Pick up two 15°s and weave through the next drop picot, then pick up two 15°s and weave through the next bicone. Repeat until the netting is complete.

5 You'll notice that there are two different kinds of gaps to fill—around the 6-mm rounds and between the fire-polished beads. Weave through the netting and fill the gaps on the left and the right side of each 6-mm round with two 15°s (the beads are outlined in red in figure 4).

Now weave forward so the thread exits a vertical fire-polished bead, toward the large gap between two 6-mm rounds. Pick up one 4-mm pearl and weave through the next vertical fire-polished bead. Repeat this step to fill all three gaps. Secure the thread and cut it off.

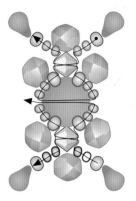

figure 3

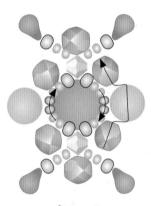

figure 4

6 Pass a head pin through the vertical center of the beadwork. If you want, place a fire-polished or other bead on the head pin, then make a wrapped loop through the loop of an ear wire. The added bead keeps the head pin snugly inside the beaded bead.

Repeat all steps to make a second earring.

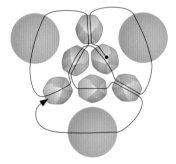

figure 1

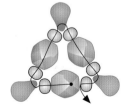

figure 2

RAW RIBS BRACELET

The base of this bracelet consists of a series of pieces of cubic RAW made from fire-polished beads, later embellished with netting. There are so many beautiful kinds of fire-polished beads that whether you use ones with matte surfaces or AB finishes, each version of this cuff can look completely different.

1 Using 4-mm fire-polished beads, make a section of RAW that's three by three units. Roll it into a tube and join the two sides with RAW as follows: Weave through the three beads at the bottom of the square, pick up one 4-mm bead, and weave again through the four beads at the base of the tube; pass up through the first vertical bead on one side (figure 1).

Pick up one 4-mm bead and pass down through the corresponding vertical bead on the opposite side. Weave through the bead added in the first row, the first vertical bead you passed through, and the bead added in this row. Weave forward so the thread exits a vertical bead in the second unit (figure 2). Continue in this manner to join the third row, then weave through the four beads on the top again.

2 Using the vertical beads in this tube, weave another section of RAW that's four units wide and three units tall. Roll this section into a tube and join the fourth unit to the second unit as described in step 1. There will be one row of units between the tubes.

3 Make another tube as described in step 2. It's very important to start the beading in the right position. When looking at the bottom (or top) of the tubes they should appear as rhombuses attached with a link in the middle, as shown in figure 3. After finishing, the base will look the same from the front and the back. Build a base of about 11 tubes as described in the previous steps.

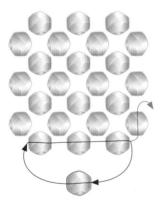

figure 1

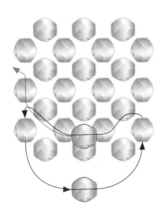

figure 2

figure 3

SUPPLIES

360 blue-green fire-polished beads, 4 mm

Size 15° seed beads, 3 g

Size 11° seed beads, 4 g

165 bronze magatama beads, 3 mm

26 violet beads, 3 mm (fire-polished beads, round beads, or crystals)

1 golden magnetic clasp

2 golden jump rings, 7.5 mm

FireLine, 6-pound test

Size 12 beading needle

Small sharp scissors

2 pairs of flat-nose pliers

FINISHED SIZE

1 x 7⅛ inches (2.5 x 18 cm), not including clasp

4 Now you'll add beads in a crisscross fashion on the front side of the tubes and the links between them. With the thread exiting a horizontal fire-polished bead at the edge of the top of the first tube and heading away from the beadwork, string one 15°, one 11°, one magatama, one 11°, and one 15°. Lay the beads diagonally over one RAW unit in the base and pass through the next horizontal fire-polished bead. Repeat two more times, exiting the corresponding horizontal bead on the bottom of the first tube. To complete the cross-stitches, string one 15° and one 11°, pass through the magatama in the last set of beads added, string on one 11° and one 15°, and pass through the next horizontal fire-polished bead. Repeat two more times until you reach the top again. Add cross-stitches on the second half of the tube (figure 4).

5 Weave along the vertical line on the front of the tube and fill the two ditches between the fire-polished beads with violet 3-mm beads. Space is tight so you'll have to push these beads into position—the beads will make the tubes curve slightly. Continue covering the base with the cross-stitches, adding ditch beads to the tubes (figure 5).

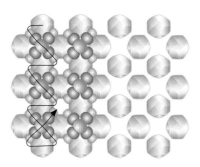

figure 4

Reverse side

6 Finally, fill the gaps on the sides of the bracelet. Fill each of the visible crossing points where you can still see the thread with one magatama.

7 Attach the clasp with jump rings, placing the rings around the vertical beads in the middle of each end of the bracelet.

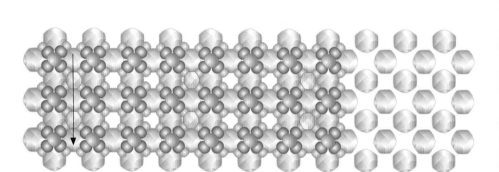

figure 5

29

GRACE BRACELET

The base of this bracelet is a simple version of RAW. The interesting zigzag shape stems from the alternation of square and triangle shapes, rather than all squares.

1 String one 4-mm fire-polished bead and one 6-mm round bead two times and weave through the four beads again to form a ring. End with the thread exiting a fire-polished bead. String two more fire-polished beads and pass through the bead from which the thread originally exited. Pass through the first fire-polished bead just added and form a RAW unit by stringing one 6-mm round, one fire-polished bead, and one 6-mm round, and passing again through the fire-polished bead from which the thread exited.

Weave forward through the newly added fire-polished bead. String two fire-polished beads and pass again through the bead from which the thread exited. Weave forward to exit the second fire-polished bead just added and begin a new RAW unit with one 6-mm round, one fire-polished bead, and one 6-mm round (figure 1). Keep beading in this fashion until the strip, which serves as the base of the bracelet, is 15 RAW units long, ending with a RAW unit.

2 For the second layer, you'll add cross-stitches above the RAW units. In the first part of the step, you'll weave along the whole length, beading half of the netting, and then complete it on the way back. Begin with the thread exiting the left side of the fire-polished bead at one end. String one 15°, one 11°, one bicone, one 11°, and one 15°; pass through the next fire-polished bead, from right to left. Weave forward so the thread exits the right side of the first fire-polished bead in the next RAW unit. Again string one 15°, one 11°, one bicone, one 11°, and one 15°. Pass through the next fire-polished bead from left to right.

Continue beading in this manner until you reach the other end of the strip. Turn back and complete the netting as follows. String one 15° and one 11° and pass through the bicone. String one 11° and one 15° and pass through the next fire-polished bead and on to the next RAW unit. Weave back along the entire strip in this way (figure 2).

SUPPLIES

30 golden round beads, 6 mm

44 green/teal fire-polished beads, 4 mm

15 jet black 2XAB crystal bicones, 3 mm

28 bright gold round beads, 3 mm

14 copper round beads, 4 mm

Size 11° dark topaz seed beads, 1 g

Size 15° light gold seed beads, 1 g

1 magnetic golden clasp, 5 mm

2 golden jump rings, 5 mm

FireLine, 6-pound test

Size 12 beading needle

Small sharp scissors

2 pairs of flat-nose pliers

FINISHED SIZE

7½ inches (19 cm), not including clasp

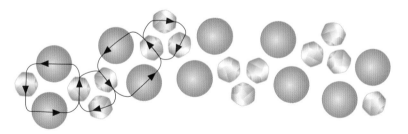

figure 1

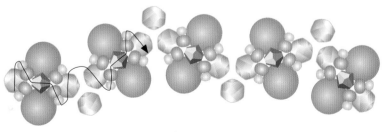

figure 2

3 In this step you'll fill the gaps at the sides of the strip where the thread shows with round beads. With the thread exiting a fire-polished bead at one end, pick up one 11° and pass through the next 6-mm round. Fill the gaps in on both sides of the fire-polished beads (the long side of the triangle of fire-polished beads) with 3-mm rounds, and fill each of the gaps at the short side of the triangle (between two 6-mm rounds) with one 4-mm round, adding one 11° to each side of the fire-polished beads on the ends (figure 3).

4 For the last layer, weave forward until the thread exits a 3-mm round in front of a fire-polished bead (long side of the triangle). String two 15°s, one 11°, and two 15°s, skip the fire-polished bead, and weave through the next 3-mm and 6-mm round beads to form an arc. String two 15°s, one 11°, and two 15°s, skip the 4-mm round, and weave through the next 6-mm and 3-mm rounds, forming another arc. Do this along both outside edges. The arcs above the fire-polished beads will flip to the outside, and the arcs above the 4-mm rounds will flip to the inside (figure 4).

5 At both ends of the beadwork, add two 15°s, one 11°, and two 15°s between the 11°s, forming an arc around the fire-polished beads at the ends. With the thread exiting the size 11° seed bead in the middle of each arc, make a loop of six 11°s; pass through the loop again and add one 15° in each of the gaps that form between the 11°s. Attach the clasp to the ending loops with jump rings.

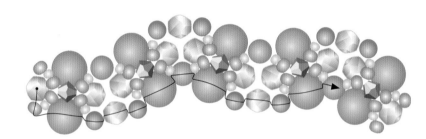

figure 3

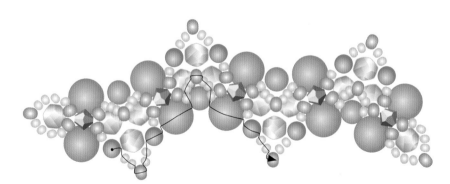

figure 4

VERTICALS BRACELET

This bracelet is made from a mix of right angle weave and ladder stitch. The vertical embellishments lend the project its name, as well as its stability. The arrangement of the bugle beads keeps the base structurally functional, but the embellishment of fringes and crystals brings a whole other level of style.

SUPPLIES

3-mm red gold bugle beads, 4 g

Size 11° bronze seed beads, 3 g

Size 15° metallic green seed beads, 3.5 g

30 copper round beads, 3 mm

30 golden-orange crystal bicones, 4 mm

1 golden lobster clasp

2 golden jump rings, 5 mm

FireLine, 6-pound test

Size 12 beading needle

Small sharp scissors

2 pairs of flat-nose pliers

FINISHED SIZE

6⅞ inches (17.5 cm), not including clasp

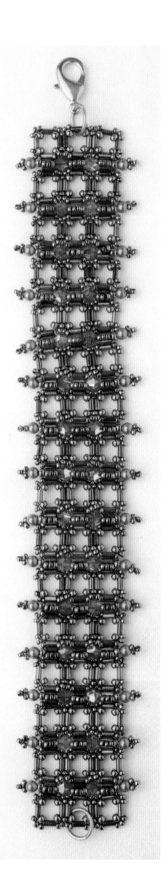

1 String one bugle bead and one size 11° seed bead; repeat three more times, for a total of eight beads on your thread. Pass through the first bead to form the basic square. Weave through the square again to secure the thread and end exiting a bugle bead.

2 String three size 15° seed beads, skip the 11° in the corner, and pass through the next bugle bead. Repeat three more times. End with the thread exiting the bugle bead on the right side (figure 1).

3 Add three bugle beads to the right side using ladder stitch as follows. *Pick up one bugle bead, pass through the bugle bead from which the thread exited, and then again through the newly added bugle bead. Repeat from * two more times. After adding three bugle beads, weave back to the basic square so that the thread exits the left side of the bugle bead on the bottom of the basic square, as shown in figure 2.

4 Add one bugle bead at the bottom of the square using ladder stitch and end with the thread exiting this newly added bead. Now start building the next square in the same way as described in the previous steps. The new square will share two 15°s with the previous square; these are outlined in red in figure 3. Add three bugle beads on the right side and add another bugle bead on the bottom of the second square, where you'll start the next square.

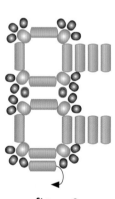

figure 2

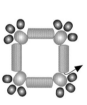

figure 1

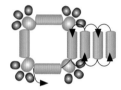

figure 3

5 After you bead the third square (here you don't add a bugle bead on the bottom!), you'll bead the vertical embellishments. You'll attach these along the two middle bugle beads in the ladder stitch units. Start at the lowest unit with the thread exiting the third bugle bead, and heading toward the outer edge. String one 11°, one round, and three 15°s, weave back through the round and the 11°, and then pass through the second bugle bead. Pick up one bicone and pass through the second bugle bead in the next unit, then pick up one bicone and pass through the second bugle in the upper ladder stitch unit. Next, string one 11°, one round, and three 15°s. Weave back through the round and the 11°, then pass through the third bugle bead. Weave along the line of bicones and the third bugle beads in the units until you reach the other side. Make a turn by weaving again through the fringe of 11°, round, and 15°s, ending with the thread exiting the size 11° seed bead in the fringe (figure 4).

6 String three 15°s, skip the bugle beads, and pass through the next bicone. String four 15°s, skip the middle group of bugle beads, pass through the second bicone, and add three more 15°s to the last gap. Weave through the fringe on top and back to the upper group of bugle beads. The thread exits the upper bugle bead on the right side (figure 5).

7 The bugle bead from which the thread exits is the left bugle bead in the next square. Build additional squares as described in the previous steps until the beadwork reaches the desired length (the version shown here has 15 squares), using the bugle beads on the right sides of the ladder-stitched grouping of four bugle beads as the bugle beads on the left of the new squares.

8 Finish the strip of beadwork with a line of squares without adding bugle beads on the right sides. Weave through the middle squares on both ends of the bracelet several times to strengthen the beadwork. Attach the clasp to these center units with jump rings.

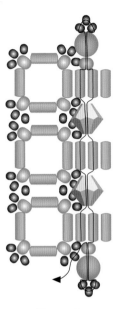

figure 4

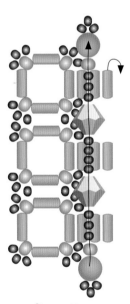

figure 5

SUPPLIES

192 copper fire-polished beads, 4 mm

21 metallic copper round beads, 6 mm

Size 15° dark bronze seed beads, 3 g

Size 11° dark bronze seed beads, 3 g

Size 8° opaque curry seed beads, 2 g

3-mm brown magatama beads, 3 g

28 red crystal bicones

2 copper jump rings, 6 mm

1 copper magnetic clasp

FireLine, 6-pound test

Size 12 beading needle

Small sharp scissors

2 pairs of flat-nose pliers

FINISHED SIZE

7½ inches (19 cm),
not including clasp

XXOXX BRACELET

After creating several more-dimensional pieces using cubic RAW, I wanted to create an embellished version of a flat RAW with not only different bead sizes but also different bead shapes in the basic lattice. The finished bracelet has a chain of little beaded cross-stitches with the loops going around the round beads, and this reminded me of the hugs and kisses symbols.

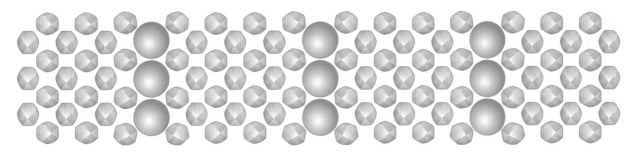

figure 1

1 Build a base of 3 x 30 units in RAW as follows. Weave two three-unit rows with fire-polished beads. Weave the next row with 6-mm round beads—instead of fire-polished beads—on the right side. Weave three more rows with fire-polished beads, then weave another with 6-mm rounds on the right side. Continue in this fashion until there are seven rows with 6-mm round beads, then add three more rows made with fire-polished beads. Figure 1 shows a part of the whole base.

2 Now you'll build cross-stitches on top of those RAW units that are made of only fire-polished beads. Starting from the horizontal fire-polished bead on one corner of the base, and with the thread exiting the left side of the bead, string one 15°, one 11°, one magatama, one 11°, and one 15°, then weave from right to left through the next horizontal fire-polished bead in this row. Repeat twice more. To complete the cross-stitches, string one 15° and one 11°, pass through the magatama bead, string one 11° and one 15°, and pass from the right to the left through the next fire-polished bead in this row. Repeat twice more to complete the row, then repeat the entire step to add cross-stitches to the next row of three units. Weave forward through the beadwork to the next two rows of RAW units that are made of only fire-polished beads and cover them with cross-stitches.

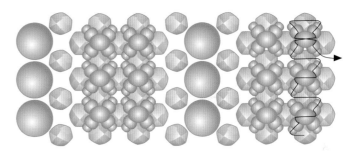

figure 2

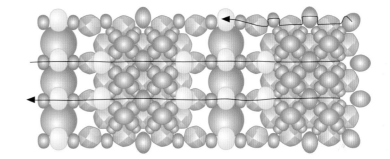

figure 3

Don't weave straight from one unit to the next or you'll cover the holes between the beads and have problems with the embellishment later on. Make sure your thread path follows the RAW (figure 2).

3 In this step you'll fill the gaps at the crossing points. To cover one line in the center of the beadwork as shown in figure 3, pass through the first horizontal fire-polished bead, *pick up one

magatama, pass through the next fire-polished bead, pick up one 8°, and pass through the next fire-polished bead. String one 11°, one 8°, and one 11° and pass through the next fire-polished bead. Pick up one 8° and pass through the next fire-polished bead. Repeat from * until you reach the other end of the strip. Turn around and fill the next center line in the same way. On the short sides (the beginning and end of the strip), fill the gaps with magatamas. Fill the long side as follows: Starting from the corner where you added one magatama, pass through the first fire-polished bead, add one magatama, and pass through the next fire-polished bead. Pick up one 11° and pass through the next fire-polished bead, string one 11°, one 8°, and one 11°; pass through the next fire-polished bead. Add one 11°

and weave through the next fire-polished bead. Continue in this fashion until the outside is completed, then repeat on the opposite edge.

4 In this step you'll add arcs above the round beads. With the thread exiting the left side of a size 8° seed bead above a round bead, string eight 15°s, skip the round bead, and pass from the left to the right through the next 8°. String eight 15°s, skip the round bead, and pass from the right to the left through the next size 8° seed bead. Complete the arcs by stringing eight 15°s and passing through the next 8°, alternating the direction from left to right then right to left through the 8°s until you return to the starting bead (figure 4). Repeat for all columns of round beads.

5 With the thread exiting an 8° seed bead between two round beads, string one bicone and three 15°s, and then weave back through the bicone and the 8°. String one bicone and three 15°s, and again weave back through the bicone and the 8°. Repeat the same steps on both sides of all 8° seed beads between the round beads, forming small fringes with picots (figure 5).

6 Weave through the center RAW units on both ends of the bracelet to strengthen them. Thread a jump ring through each unit and add half the clasp to each jump ring.

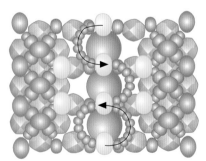

figure 4

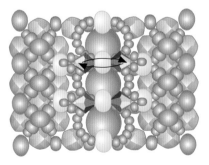

figure 5

Alternate Colorway

CHAPTER 3
BEZELED STONES

A stone needs to be attached firmly so it can't drop out of its bezel, but you want it to show as much as possible. In this chapter, you'll learn my solutions to this challenge. Here's one trick: Surround a rivoli with other sparkling crystals to highlight its shimmer.

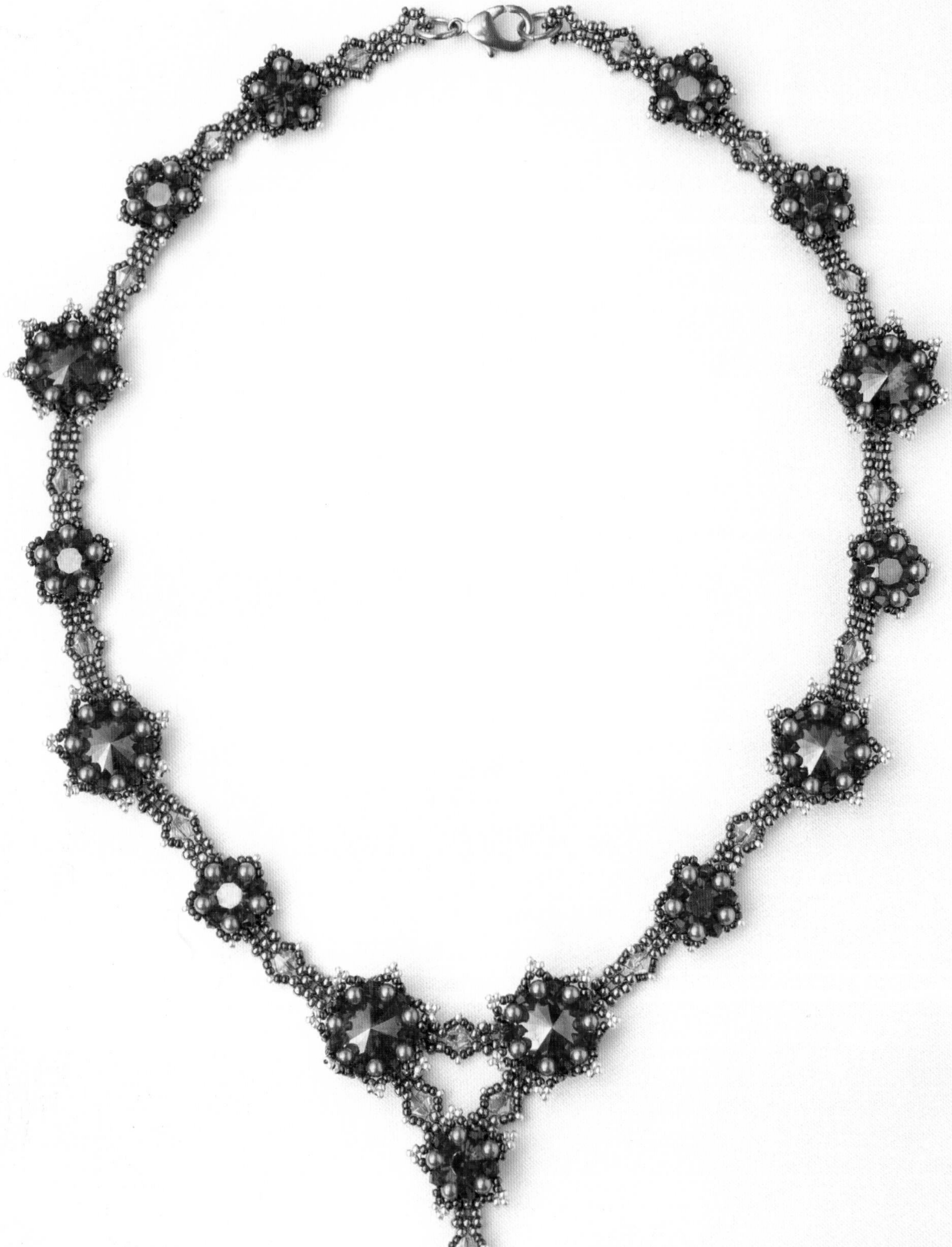

LES FLEURS NECKLACE

This necklace is made of little flowers in two different sizes. Simply combine them any way you like. The overall V shape creates a perfect fit because the links between the flowers are straight. After building a flower, connect it with a link to the previous ones. All the links are made in the same way, except for those in the middle, which are a bit shorter.

▶ Overview

The flowers are joined with links of 11° seed beads that are worked from a ring of seed beads on the back side of the flowers. The small flowers have a ring of 10 size 11° beads, and you can work the link from any of them. Just make sure the flowers are linked in the same position. The large flowers end with a ring of five arcs with one 11° between six 15°s, and you'll work the links from one of the 11°s. Because there is an odd number of arcs, the necklace will curve—you'll have one more arc between the links on the outside of the curve than on the inside.

The instructions for making the Small Flowers, the Large Flowers, the Long Links, and the Short Links appear below. Bead the flowers and links in the following order:

• Make a Small Flower with a Long Link with a loop of seven size 11° seed beads. This loop will be used to attach one half of the clasp.

• Make another Small Flower and add it to the previous one with a Long Link.

• Make a Large Flower and add it to the previous flower with a Long Link.

• Make a Small Flower and add it to the previous flower with a Long Link (three arcs on the back side of the Large Flower on one side and two arcs on the other side).

SUPPLIES

87 copper glass pearls, 3 mm

87 red crystal bicones, 3 mm

Size 15° seed beads:

Dark bronze, 5 g

Golden, 4 g

Size 11° bronze seed beads, 8 g

9 deep red chatons, 8 mm

6 deep red rivolis, 14 mm

18 pale beige AB crystal bicones, 4 mm

2 copper split rings, 6 mm

1 copper lobster clasp, 7 mm

FireLine, smoke, 6-pound test

Size 12 beading needle

Small sharp scissors

2 pairs of flat-nose pliers

FINISHED SIZE

18 inches (45.7 cm), not including clasp

A large flower flanked by small flowers

- Make another Large Flower and add it to the previous flower with a Long Link.

- Make a Small Flower with a Long Link and add it to the previous Large Flower, taking care that the two- and three-arc sides are positioned as for the previous Large Flower—there will be two arcs on the inside and three arcs on the outside.

- Make another Large Flower with a Long Link. This is the first of the three flowers in the centerpiece.

- Add a Small Flower with a Short Link, but this time place two units of the Large Flower on the outside and three units on the inside.

- Make another Large Flower with a Short Link and attach it to the top of the Small Flower of the centerpiece, right next to the other link on this flower.

Make the rest of the necklace by reversing the order previously described, mirroring the first half. There's an additional Short Link between the two Large Flowers in the centerpiece and half a Short Link at the bottom of the Small Flower (figure 1).

▶ Small Flower

1 Refer to figure 2 for steps 1 through 3. String one round bead and one 3-mm bicone; repeat four more times, for a total of 10 beads strung. Pass through the first bead strung to create a ring, and weave twice through all the beads to secure the thread. The thread exits a round bead.

figure 1

figure 2

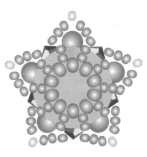

figure 3

2 String four dark bronze 15°s and pass again through the round bead, forming an arc. Pass through the next bicone, string six dark bronze 15°s, and pass again through the bicone, forming another arc, then pass through the next round bead. Repeat these steps until you've beaded around the entire ring. At the end of the row, weave forward so the thread exits the second bead in the first group of four 15°s added in this row.

3 Pick up one golden 15°; weave through the third and fourth 15°s in this arc and the first three 15°s in the next arc. Pick up one 11° and weave forward until you reach the middle of the next arc of four size 15° seed beads. Repeat these steps until you've beaded your way around the entire ring (outlined in red in figure 2). At the end, weave forward so the thread exits a size 11° seed bead.

4 Pick up one 11° and pass through the 11° in the next arc above the next bicone. Repeat four more times, then pass again through the 11° from which the thread exited. Pull the thread to form a ring of the 11°s; all the large arcs are connected to this ring. This is the back side of the bezel. Loosen the thread and place one chaton face down into the bezel. Again pull the thread up tight and weave

several times through the ten 11°s to secure the thread (figure 3). The links are worked from and attached to this ring of ten 11°s on the back of the bezel.

▶ **Large Flower**

1 This flower is beaded in the same way as the Small Flower, but the bead count is a bit different. For the first row string one 3-mm bicone and one round bead; repeat six more times for a total of 14 beads on your thread. Form a ring as in Small Flower step 1.

2 Build the smaller arcs (four dark bronze 15°s) at the round beads and the larger arcs (six dark bronze 15°s) at the bicones as described in Small Flower step 2. In the next step, add *three* golden 15°s in the middle of the small arcs (not one as shown for the Small Flower) and one 11° in the middle of the large arcs. The thread exits the size 11° seed bead of a large arc.

String three 11°s and pass through the size 11° in the next arc above the next bicone. Repeat six more times to complete the ring. Place the rivoli face down in the bezel, and weave through all the beads in the ring of 11°s to secure the thread. End with the thread exiting the middle 11° in a set of three added in the last row.

Small flower

3 Pick up one 11° (outlined in green in figure 4), skip three beads, and weave through the fourth (this is the middle of the next set of three 11°s added in the last row). Repeat six more times. End with the thread exiting the first bead added in this row.

Pick up two golden 15°s and pass through the next 11° added in the previous row. Repeat six more times. Weave several times through the beads of the last row to secure the thread.

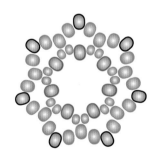

figure 4

► Long Links

The links are made with a variation of RAW stitch. Note that the 11° seed bead at the beginning and the end of the links is also one bead on the back side of the flowers (outlined in red in figure 5).

1 Refer to figure 5 for this step. Bead two units of RAW using 11°s. For the next unit, string one 11°, one 4-mm bicone, and three 11°s; pass back through the bicone, pick up one 11°, and pass again through the 11° seed bead from which the thread exited at the beginning of this step. Weave forward so the thread exits the middle 11°

seed bead in the group of three on the other side of the bicone. Add two more units of RAW made of 11°s.

2 Weave along the exterior of this link and (starting from the seed bead shared with the flower) add between the beads one golden 15°, one size 11° twice, and four dark bronze 15°s at the bicone, then one size 11° twice and one golden 15° (beads are outlined in black in figure 6). Repeat on the other side of the link. Weave a second time along the exterior and add one golden 15° in the middle of the four dark bronze 15°s (outlined in green in figure 6).

► Short Links

Follow Long Links steps 1 and 2 to build the Short Links, but begin and end with one unit (not two) of RAW made from 11°s. To make the half link at the bottom of the centerpiece, start with two units in RAW, but don't add RAW units after the bicone (just the three beads as shown in figure 5).

► Attach the Clasp

Add a jump ring to one of the seven-bead loops and use the other jump ring to attach the clasp to the other seven-bead loop.

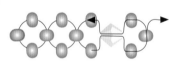

figure 5

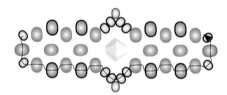

figure 6

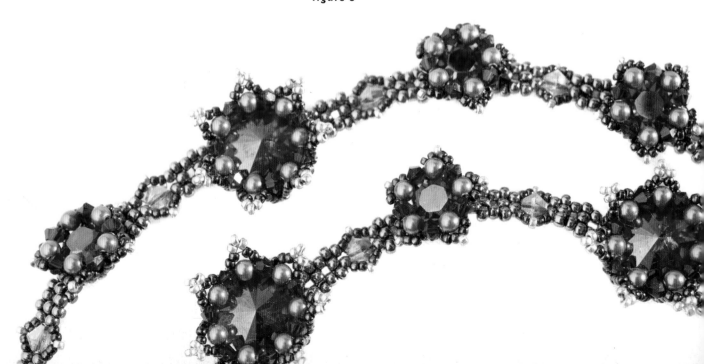

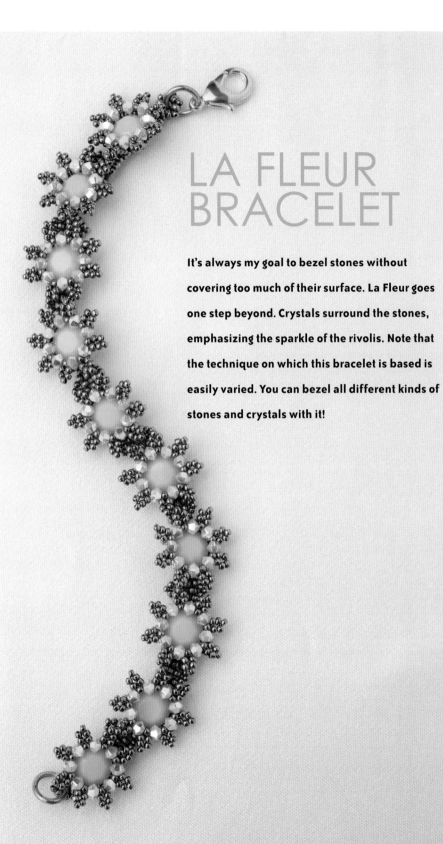

LA FLEUR BRACELET

It's always my goal to bezel stones without covering too much of their surface. La Fleur goes one step beyond. Crystals surround the stones, emphasizing the sparkle of the rivolis. Note that the technique on which this bracelet is based is easily varied. You can bezel all different kinds of stones and crystals with it!

SUPPLIES

10 milky mint-green chatons, 8 mm

80 milky mint-green 2XAB crystal bicones, 3 mm

Size 11° bronze seed beads, 2 g

Size 15° bronze seed beads, 6 g

2 jump rings, 5 mm

1 golden lobster clasp, 10 mm

FireLine, 6-pound test

Size 12 beading needle

Small sharp scissors

2 pairs of flat-nose pliers

FINISHED SIZE

6⅞ inches (17.5 cm), not including clasp

1 String one size 15° seed bead and one bicone. Repeat seven times, for a total of 16 beads on your thread, then pass through the first bead strung to create a ring. Weave twice through the whole ring to secure the thread. End with the thread exiting a bicone (figure 1).

2 String six 15°s and pass through the bicone from which the thread exited to form an arc of beads above the bicone, then pass through the next 15° in the ring (figure 2). String two 15°s and again pass through the 15° from which the thread originally exited to form a small arc, and then weave through the next bicone in the ring (figure 3). Repeat the two steps until you've gone completely around the ring. Weave forward through the first three 15°s in the first arc so the thread exits in the middle of the arc.

3 Pick up one size 11° seed bead and weave through the next three 15°s in this arc, then through the first 15° in the next small arc. String three 15°s and weave through the second 15° in the small arc, then continue through the first three beads in the next larger arc. The three 15°s added to the small arcs should be pushed into a triangular shape by pulling the middle one of the three beads out each time you add the beads. Continue adding beads in this fashion until you've beaded around the entire ring. End with the thread exiting the 11° added to the first arc (figure 4).

4 Pick up one 15° and pass through the 11° in the next arc. Continue adding beads in this fashion around the entire ring, then pass again through the 11° bead originally exited in this round. Pull the thread to close the ring, then loosen it again and put the chaton into the bezel, upside-down, with the front of the chaton framed by the bicones. Tighten the thread again and weave several times through the last ring of beads until the thread is firmly secured (figure 5).

Repeat steps 1 through 4 to make nine more bezeled chatons, attaching each unit to the previous one when it is finished, as described in steps 5 and 6.

figure 1

figure 2

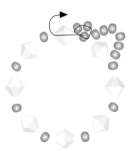

figure 3

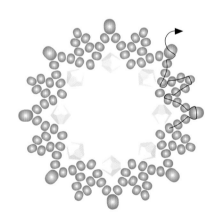

figure 4

5 To attach the bezeled chatons to each other, build links in RAW, starting from an 11° bead in the last round. Be sure to use opposing beads to attach the links, to keep the bezels lying in a straight line. Build a link of three units in RAW between two bezels using 11° seed beads; the beads in the last round, on the back side of the bezels, are outlined in red in figure 6.

6 Weave through the link and fill the gaps with one 15° seed bead both before and after the starting beads of the bezels, and with 11° seed beads between the RAW units on both sides (outlined in black in figure 7). Weave forward so the thread exits the 11° seed bead right before the center of the link. String three 15°s (outlined in green in figure 7), skip the 11° seed bead in the middle, and pass through the next 11° seed bead. Weave through the beadwork to the other side and add three 15°s here in the manner previously

described. Use these additional turns through the beadwork to secure the links to the bezeled chatons—meaning that as long as you can pass through the beads, always weave through the whole link and don't take any shortcuts.

7 At both ends of the strip of linked bezels, create a loop of seven size 11° seed beads. Pass through the loop again and add 15°s in the four gaps between the 11°s. Attach a jump ring to each loop, and attach the lobster clasp to one jump ring.

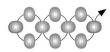

figure 6

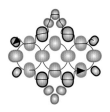

figure 7

47

figure 5

Reverse side

QUEENIE
BRACELET

It has always bugged me that when you bezel a rivoli, you're covering wide swaths of its beauty with other beads! So I mulled it over. When a jeweler mounts a diamond, the setting allows light to shine into it from all sides. My goal was to create a bezel that made this possible. Mechanically speaking, size 6° seed beads work like holders for the rivolis; they are forced into position by the beads that surround them. It's therefore important as you work to really secure the basic ring of the bezel and maintain proper thread tension.

1 For the basic ring, string one 11°, two cylinder beads, one 11°, one 6°, one 11°, and two cylinder beads. Repeat this sequence three more times, for a total of 32 beads on the thread. Pass through the first bead strung to create a ring, and weave three more times through the entire ring. The thread should be really secure—you should not be able to pull it out of the beads. (Later, the bezel will take on the shape of a square, but for now, it's a ring.) To orient ourselves, let's call the size 6° seed beads corner beads. The thread exits a cylinder bead in front of a size 11° seed bead at the center of one side of the square.

2 String one cylinder, one 11°, and one cylinder; skip the 11° and weave through the next two cylinders and through one 11°, forming a picot. String four 15°s, skip the size 6° bead (a corner bead), and weave through the next 11° and two cylinders. Repeat three more times. Exit from the next size 11° bead in the basic ring, at the center of one side of the square (figure 1).

3 String one 15°, one 11°, and one bicone, then weave through the first two 15°s at the corner. Pick up one 15° and weave through the next two 15°s; string one bicone, one 11°, and one 15°; pass through the size 11° seed bead at the center of the next side of the square. Repeat three more times. When you're finished, weave to the back side so the thread exits a size 11° seed bead—one that's part of a picot added in step 2, shown with a dot in figure 2.

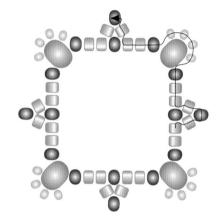

figure 1

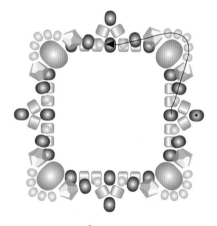

figure 2

SUPPLIES

Size 11° galvanized rose
seed beads, 4 g

Size 11° gold-lined aqua
cylinder beads, 2 g

49 size 6° bronze seed beads

Size 15° galvanized light gold
seed beads, 1 g

56 clear with bronze effect 2X
crystal bicones

7 brown rivolis, 14 mm

2 copper jump rings, 6 mm

1 copper lobster clasp,
½ inch (1.3 cm)

FireLine, 6-pound test

Size 12 beading needle

Small sharp scissors

2 pairs of flat-nose pliers

FINISHED SIZE

6¾ inches (17.1 cm)

Reverse side

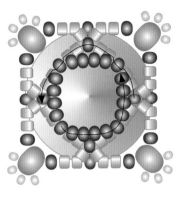

figure 3

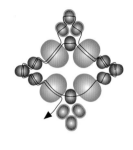

figure 4

4 As you work steps 4 and 5, refer to figure 3. On the back side of the bezel, string two cylinders, one 11°, and two cylinders; pass through the 11° bead in the next picot. Repeat three more times. Place the rivoli into the bezel with the back point centered in the newly formed ring of beads, and pull the thread tight. Weave twice more through the beads in this ring until the thread is secured. End with the thread exiting a size 11° seed bead added in this row.

5 String four 11°s and weave through the next size 11° added in step 4. Repeat three more times, then weave several times through the new ring of 11°s to secure the thread. End with the thread exiting an 11° bead in a picot added in step 2 (outlined in green in figure 3).

6 Repeat steps 1 through 5 to bead a second component and link it to the first component as follows. With the thread exiting an 11° bead as instructed in step 5, string one 11°, one 6°, one 11°, one 6°, and one 11°; pass through the corresponding 11° bead in the previous unit. String the same bead count again and pass through the 11° bead originally exited at the beginning of this step. Weave again through the beads in this ring and end with the thread exiting a size 6° bead in front of a single 11°, as shown in figure 4 (continue to refer to this illustration as you work the next step).

7 Pick up three 11°s, pass through the next size 6°, forming a picot, and weave forward to the opposite side. Add another three 11°s (outlined in green in figure 4), then weave several times through the beads in the link to secure the thread.

8 Repeat steps 1 through 7 until you have seven components joined by six links. At both ends of the bracelet, make a loop to attach the clasp, as follows. With the thread exiting the 11° opposite the last link, string five 11°s and again pass through the bead originally exited. Weave again through the loop, adding four 15°s in the gaps between the 11°s. Weave through all beads of the loop again to strengthen. Attach one half of the clasp to each loop using jump rings.

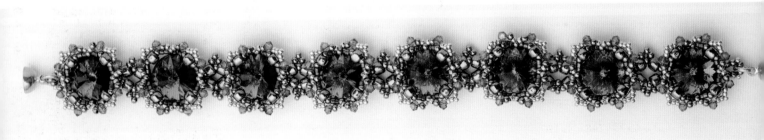

Alternate Colorway

MEDAL PENDANT

A gold-colored version of this pendant, shown on page 55, was the first piece I made after I was asked to pitch the idea for what eventually became this book. Of all the outstanding beaders in the world, Lark Jewelry & Beading was considering me! After making Medal Pendant, I posted its picture on my blog. It was my very own private reward, to celebrate my secret success. Although the book deal was uncertain and I had to keep the negotiations to myself, putting the image up on my site was a way to signal the world, even though I was the only one who knew the real reason. The final purple version that was ultimately chosen as the project turned out to be even more spectacular than the original.

SUPPLIES

Size 11° black cylinder beads, 3 g

Size 11° dark bronze seed beads, 3 g

Size 15° iris gold seed beads, 2 g

1 fuchsia-purple chaton, 27 mm

4 rose 2XAB rivolis, 8 mm

23 light red AB satin crystal bicones, 3 mm

1 rose drop pearl, 6 x 11 mm

1 golden head pin

2 golden jump rings

FireLine, smoke, 6-pound test

Size 12 beading needle

Small sharp scissors

2 pairs of flat-nose pliers

Round-nose pliers

FINISHED SIZE

4 inches (10.2 cm) long

Reverse side

▶ Bezel the Chaton

1 Although this bezel is very small on the front, it's important to cover most of the back side, or the stone may fall out. String three cylinder beads and one 11° seed bead; repeat 15 more times for a total of 64 beads on your thread. Pass through the first bead strung to create a ring. Weave through all the beads to secure the thread, exiting in front of a size 11° seed bead.

2 Pick up one 11° and weave through the next three cylinder beads. Repeat 15 more times as you work your way completely around the ring. Stitch forward so the thread exits in front of the size 11° seed beads. It's important to maintain good thread tension, especially in this first round.

3 String three 15°s and weave through the next three cylinder beads. The three 15°s form a little picot. Repeat, beading completely around the ring. At the end, weave through the beadwork so the thread exits an 11° added in step 2.

4 For the next round, string one cylinder, two 15°s, and one cylinder; pass through the next 11°. Repeat to bead your way around the entire ring. Weave forward so the thread exits a cylinder bead in front of a size 11° seed bead.

5 Pick up one 11° and weave through the next four beads (one cylinder, two 15°s, and one cylinder). Repeat until the ring is complete beaded.

6 In the next round, add three cylinder beads between the size 11° seed beads.

7 Now add one 11° between the groups of three cylinder beads added in step 6. Place the chaton upside-down into the bezel. It's not secure at this point because the ring is still too flexible; adding several rounds on the back side will secure the stone in place. There are several ways to cover the back. I use a mix of peyote and netting.

8 Add two size 15° seed beads in the first gap, and two cylinder beads in the next. These beads are outlined in red in figure 1. Continue like this to complete the round, then bead another round with size 11° seed beads in the gaps.

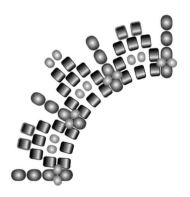

figure 1

9 Start the netting as follows: Add one 15°, one 11°, and one 15° in the gaps. At the end of the round, weave forward so the thread exits the 11° seed bead in the first group of three beads. Pick up one 11° and pass through the 11° seed bead in the next group of three beads. Continue like this until the circle is complete. You'll have 16 size 11°s in the last round.

10 To reduce the number of 11°s in the next round, string three 11°s, skip three beads (instead of one bead) from the previous round, and pass through the next bead. This decreases the number of units in this round from 16 to eight. In the next (and also last) round, add one 11° between the middle of three beads, as you did in the second part of step 9.

Weave through the beadwork so the thread exits the beads in the fourth round (a group of one cylinder bead, two 15°s, and one cylinder bead). Weave along the beads in this round and add one 11° between each group of four beads (add the 11°s between two cylinders). Feel to make sure the bezel is stiff and the stone is secure; if it's not, pass through all the beads in this round again. End with the thread exiting the first bead added in this round.

11 String four cylinder beads and pass through the next 11° in the last round—this is the center bottom of the pendant where one bezeled rivoli will be placed. *String two 15°s, one bicone, and two 15°s, and pass through the next 11°; repeat from * five more times. **String four cylinder beads and pass through the next 11°; repeat from ** two more times—this is the top center of the pendant where three bezeled rivolis will be placed. Now add six units of two 15°s, one bicone, and two 15°s as for the other side.

12 Weave through the beadwork to exit the 15° before the first bicone added in step 11. String four 15°s and weave through the two 15°s after the bicone, the next 11°, and the two 15°s before the next bicone. Repeat to add arcs of four 15°s above the six bicones on this side. When you reach the center top, simply weave through the beads in the previous row without adding any beads. Repeat to add 15°s above the bicones on the other side of the bezel. Secure the thread and cut off the extra (figure 2).

▶ **Bezel the Rivolis**

You'll add four rivolis: One will be attached to the space at the bottom of the bezeled chaton and three will be attached to the space at the top.

1 Refer to figure 3 when working steps 1 through 3. The bezels will be squarish, with a short side on top, a long side on the bottom, and two medium sides on the left and right. String three cylinder beads, one 11°, four cylinders, one 11°, five cylinders, one 11°, four cylinders, and one 11°. Pass through the first bead strung to create a ring. Weave again through all the beads in the ring, exiting in front of a size 11° seed bead. As you did for the large bezel, pass through the cylinders and add one 11° at each corner and then three 15°s at each corner in the next row.

2 Add three cylinder beads between the corners of the short side; add two cylinders, one 15°, and two cylinders between the corners of the left and right sides; add two cylinder beads, one 11°, and two cylinder beads between the corners of the long side.

3 Work another row, adding size 11° seed beads at the corners. Add one last row with one 11° between the corners of the short side and three cylinder beads between the corners of the other sides. Loosen the thread and place a rivoli into the bezel. Pull the thread tightly and weave several times through the last row of beads to secure the thread (figure 3).

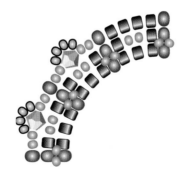

figure 2

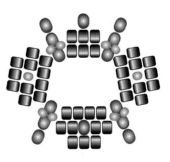

figure 3

4 Weave back to the beads in the fourth row. Add one 11° in front of and after the short side and three 11°s in front of and after the long side. The beads in the fourth row are shown with a green outline in figure 4.

5 Continue referring to figure 4. Add one 15°, one cylinder bead, one bicone, one cylinder bead, and one 15° to both the left and the right sides; add one 15°, one

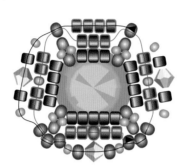

figure 4

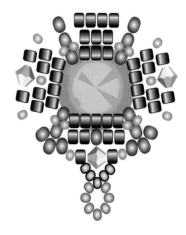

figure 5

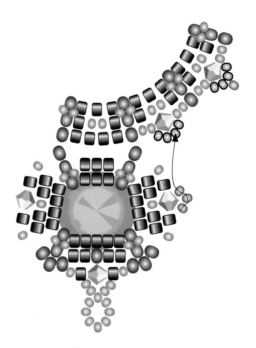

figure 6

11°, one bicone, one 11°, and one 15° to the long side. Don't add new beads to the short side, but weave through the four cylinder beads at the placement point on the bottom of the bezeled chaton (outlined in red in the illustration).

6 Repeat steps 1 through 5 to bezel three more rivolis, attaching them to the placement points at the top of the bezeled chaton. **Note:** When working step 5 for the three rivolis that are placed at the top, the center bezel shares five beads (one 15°, one 11°, one bicone, one 11°, and one 15°) with the adjacent units on each side.

7 Weave along the outside of the long side of each rivoli unit and add five 15°s to form an arc on top of the bicones (outlined in black in figure 5). At the single small rivoli unit on the pendant's bottom and on the middle of the three units on the top, add a loop of seven 15°s. (The beads in the loop are outlined in green.) Weave again through the loop, adding four more 15°s in the gaps, then weave through the beads in the loop once more to secure it.

8 Weave to the outside of the beadwork so the thread exits in front of the bicone at the side of the bottom rivoli. String three or four 15°s and weave through the third and fourth 15°s in the arc above the first bicone of the chaton bezel. Weave forward to add one 15° at the centers of the arcs of 15°s above the next four bicones in the chaton bezel (the added beads are outlined in green in figure 6), then add three or four 15°s to join the last arc to the side of the top rivoli. Repeat on the other side of the pendant.

▶ Drop Bead

1 String the drop pearl and one bicone on the head pin, make a loop on the end of the pin, and cut off the extra wire.

2 Open a jump ring and attach it to the loop at the bottom of the pendant, catching the loop of the head pin before you close it.

Attach the other jump ring to the loop at the top of the pendant and use it to hang the pendant from a chain.

PETIT CARRÉ CHOKER

The Petit Carré is a very versatile pattern. A special bezel shows as much as possible of the sparkling surface of the tiny rivolis, and the embellished links allow many variations for attaching the components. Whether you use the sparkling units to build a spectacular choker, tiny earrings, a large cuff, or a narrow bracelet, the possibilities are wide open.

1 String one bicone, one 15°, one round, and one 15°; repeat three more times for a total of 16 beads on your thread, then pass through the first bead strung and pull the thread to form a ring. Weave twice through the beads to secure the thread. This forms the base ring. End with the thread exiting a bicone (figure 1).

2 String six 15°s and pass again through the bicone from which the thread originally exited, forming an arc around the bicone. Weave through the next 15° and round bead. String four 15°s and pass again through the round bead, forming an arc, then weave forward through the next 15° and bicone. Continue around the rest of the ring in this fashion, ending with the thread exiting the third of the six size 15° seed beads above the first bicone (figure 2).

3 Pick up one 11°, weave through the next three 15°s, skip the 15° in the base ring, and weave through the first two 15°s in the next arc of four beads. Pick up one 11°, weave through the next two 15°s, skip the 15° in the base ring, and weave through the first three 15°s in the next arc of six beads. Repeat these steps around the ring, ending with the thread exiting the first 11° added in this step (figure 3).

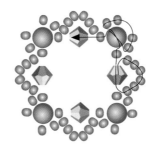

figure 2

SUPPLIES

200 olive-green 2XAB crystal bicones, 3 mm

Size 15° metallic green seed beads, 10 g

136 dark gray round beads, 3 mm

Size 11° smoky pewter seed beads, 17 g

34 blue-green rivolis, 8 mm

1 silver oval clasp, ¾ inch (1.9 cm)

2 silver jump rings, 6 mm

FireLine, 6-pound test

Size 12 beading needle

Small sharp scissors

2 pairs of flat-nose pliers

FINISHED SIZE

13¾ inches (35 cm), not including clasp

57

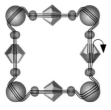

figure 1

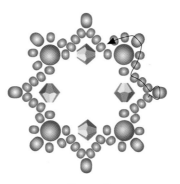

figure 3

4 In this step, you'll attach the rivoli inside the bezel and flip the arcs above the bicones to the back. Pick up one 11°, skip the smaller arc around the round bead, and pass through the 11° of the arc around the next bicone. Repeat three more times to join all arcs above the bicones. Weave through the bead originally exited and tighten the thread to pull the arcs to the back. Loosen the thread and, working from the back side, place the rivoli into the bezel, upside-down. Hold the bezel with the rivoli flat between your thumb and index finger, then pull the thread to secure the bezel. Weave several times through the beads in the last row to secure the thread (figure 4).

5 Repeat steps 1 through 4 to bead a second bezeled rivoli, ending with the thread exiting an 11° on the back side of the bezeled rivoli (not any of the ones that were added in the previous step, but the ones that are part of the larger arcs, which were flipped to the back; these are outlined in red in figure 5). Bead two units in RAW using 11°s, then one unit with one round, one 11°, and one round. Bead one unit of 11°s and another unit of 11°s that

includes the size 11° from the back side of the previously bezeled rivoli (outlined in red in figure 5), linking the bezels together. Weave along the sides of the RAW units just added, filling each of the four gaps with one 11° (outlined in black in figure 5). Weave forward so the thread exits an 11° in front of a round bead. String four 15°s, skip the round bead, and pass through the 11° in back of the round bead. Weave forward to the opposite side and repeat, adding four 15°s around the other round bead. Again weave forward to the opposite side and end with the thread exiting the middle of the first group of four size 15°s just added. Pick up one 11° and weave through the next two size 15°s. Repeat on the opposite side.

6 Bead two more bezeled rivolis and link them to the previous two-bezel component so that they make a square (the fourth rivoli will be added with two links). Weave through the beadwork so that the thread exits a size 11° (part of the arc above the round bead of the link) at the middle of the square. String one 15°, one 11°, one bicone, one 11°, and one 15°; pass through the 11° of the next link (the added beads are outlined in black in figure 6). Repeat three more times. Weave through the beads of this row again to secure the thread. End with the thread exiting an 11° seed bead in front of a bicone. String four 15°s, skip the bicone, and weave along through the 11° behind the bicone (forming an arc), then through

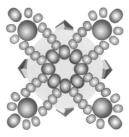

figure 4

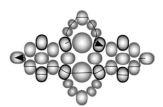

figure 5

the next 15°, 11°, 15°, and 11° seed beads (the added beads are outlined in green in figure 6). Repeat three more times to complete the ring. Weave forward so the thread exits the second bead of the first arc of 15°s just added. Pick up one 11°, then weave forward to the middle of the arc above the next bicone. Add another size 11° seed bead. Repeat two more times. Now the first unit is finished.

7 Continue beading two-bezel components as outlined in steps 1 through 5 and linking them to the previous components as described in step 6 until you have a total of 17 linked two-bezel units. At each end of the necklace, build a loop for attaching the clasp, as follows. With the thread exiting the 11° in the center of the component, string five 11°s and pass through the bead originally exited to form a ring. Pass through the ring again, adding four 15°s in the gaps between the 11°s. Pass through all beads twice more to strengthen the loop. Attach the clasp to the loops with jump rings.

figure 6

FLORAL CASCADE CHOKER

This choker includes three different bezels for rivolis and two
bezel-like elements that are left empty. They're arranged into a cascade of
flowers attached to a RAW band. Because you can improvise the colors in
the cascades at will, I've only approximated the list of supplies.

▶ Choker

1 You'll start by beading the choker, which consists of three connected rows of embellished RAW. In steps 1 and 2, use golden 11° seed beads unless told otherwise. Bead one unit of RAW. Weave again through the beads in this unit, then build a loop of five seed beads on one side of the unit. Weave twice through the beads in this loop, then stitch forward so the thread exits the opposite side of the first unit. String one 11°, one 4-mm pearl, and three 11°s; pass back through the pearl, pick up one 11°, and pass again through the bead from which the thread originally exited. Weave forward so the thread exits the middle of the three seed beads on the other side of the pearl (figure 1).

2 Make another RAW unit, then again string one 11°, one 4-mm pearl, and three 11°s; pass back through the pearl. Pick up one more 11° and pass again through the bead from which the thread exited. Continue in this fashion until you've beaded 28 units with pearls. At the end of this strip, create another loop of five 11° seed beads. **Note:** The strip will shrink a bit after attaching the next rows.

3 Weave through the loop beads and add one green 15° between the 11° seed beads as shown in figure 2, four beads total. Now weave through the outer beads on one side of the strip, adding a bronze 11° between the golden 11°s of the RAW units; when you reach a pearl, string one bronze 11°, two green 15°s, and one bronze 11°; skip the pearl and pass through the next 11°, forming an arc above the pearl. Continue in this manner along the whole side, then repeat on the other side of the strip. Finally, weave again through both sides of the strip, adding one bronze 11° in the middle of the arcs above the pearls (outlined in black in figure 2).

figure 1

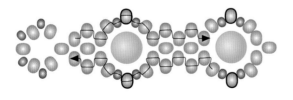

figure 2

SUPPLIES

Size 11° seed beads:
- Golden, 16 g
- Bronze, 18 g

Size 15° seed beads:
- Green, 10 g
- Golden, 10 g

56 greenish brown glass pearls, 4 mm

28 palest brown AB crystal bicones, 4 mm

220 olive green AB crystal bicones, 3 mm

210 greenish brown glass pearls, 3 mm

10 golden brown rivolis, 8 mm

10 magenta-yellow rivolis, 10 mm

10 blue-green-yellow rivolis, 14 mm

2 golden 3-strand endpieces

2 golden jump rings, 6 mm

5 golden jump rings, 5 mm

2 inches (5.1 cm) of golden chain, 3 mm

Small golden pendant

1 golden lobster clasp

FireLine, 6-pound test

Size 12 beading needle

Small sharp scissors

2 pairs of flat-nose pliers

FINISHED SIZE

Length of choker (not including metal findings), 14 inches (35.5 cm)

Length of longest central fringe, 6 inches (15.2 cm)

4 Repeat steps 1 through 3 to make a second strip, but use 4-mm bicones instead of 4-mm pearls, and in the last row of embellishment, instead of adding new bronze 11° beads in the middle of the arcs, weave through the corresponding 11°s on one side of the previous strip to connect the two strips.

5 Build a third strip just like the first, and attach it to the second strip in the last row of embellishment as described in step 4.

▶ Floral Fringe

Next you'll bead the flower-embellished fringe. You'll start from the bottom of the fringes, go on to bead the flowers and links, and then add them to the choker at the last link. You'll bead five different flower designs, but before you start working, take a look at the photograph to see how the flowers are arranged and connected. Some flowers are made with golden 15°s and others with green 15°s for different results.

Flower 1

Refer to figure 3 for all steps. String one 3-mm bicone and one golden 11°; repeat four more times for 10 beads on your thread. Pass through the first bead strung to form a ring, then weave through the beads again to secure the thread. End with the thread exiting the first 11° bead.

*String four green 15°s and pass again through the 11°, forming an arc. Pass through the next bicone. String four 15°s and pass again through the bicone, forming an arc, then pass through the next 11°. Repeat from * until you've worked your way around the ring; end with the thread exiting the second of the four beads in the first arc.

**Pick up one golden 11° and weave forward through the next four 15°s, exiting in the middle of the next arc. Add one green 15° and weave through the next four 15°s. Repeat from ** until you've beaded around the entire ring. End with the thread exiting the first 11° bead added in this row.

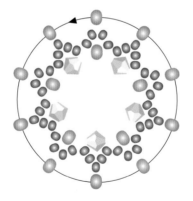

figure 3

Pick up one bronze 11°, skip the arc of 15°s, and weave through the 11° in the next arc. Repeat four more times. Weave several times through the beads in this last row to secure the thread.

Flower 1

Flower 2

Flower 2

Make this flower in the same way as Flower 1, but use 3-mm pearls instead of bicones and golden 15° seed beads instead of green.

Flower 3

Refer to figure 4. String one 3-mm bicone and one golden 15°; repeat seven more times for a total of 16 beads on your thread, then pass through the first bead strung to form a ring. Weave again through all the beads and end with the thread exiting a size 15° seed bead.

*String four green 15°s and pass again through the 15° from which the thread exited, forming an arc, then pass through the next bicone. String four golden 15°s, weave through the bicone again to form an arc, then pass through the next seed bead. Repeat from * seven more times, working your way around the entire ring. In the next row add one golden 15° in the middle of the golden arcs and one green 15° in the middle of the green arcs (these beads are outlined in black in figure 4). End with the thread exiting the first green 15° added in this row.

Pick up one bronze 11°, skip the arc of golden 15°s, and pass through the green 15° in the middle of the next arc. Repeat seven more times. Stitch forward through the first 15° seed bead added in this row. Pull the thread to flip the arcs to the back.

Loosen the thread and place an 8-mm rivoli upside-down into the bezel you've formed. Pull the thread again and weave several times through the last row of beads to secure the thread.

Flower 4

Follow along with figure 5. String one golden 11° and one 3-mm pearl; repeat seven times for a total of 16 beads on the thread. Pass through the first bead strung to make a ring, then weave through the beads again to secure the thread. End with the thread exiting a size 11° seed bead.

*String six green 15°s and pass again through the 11° from which the thread originally exited, forming an arc, then pass through the next pearl. String four golden 15°s and pass again through the pearl, forming an arc, then pass through the next 11°. Repeat from * seven more times until you've beaded around the entire ring. In the next row add one bronze 11° in the middle of the arc of six green 15°s, and add one golden 15° in the middle of the arc of four golden 15° beads. End with the thread exiting the bronze 11° added to the first arc.

**Pick up one golden 11°, skip the arc of 11°s, then pass through the 11° in the middle of the next arc. Repeat from ** seven more times. Place one 10-mm rivoli upside-down into the bezel you've formed and pull the thread. Weave several times through the last row of beads to secure the thread.

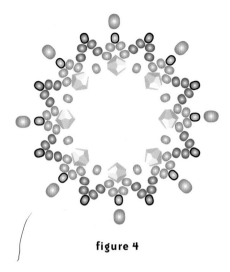

figure 4

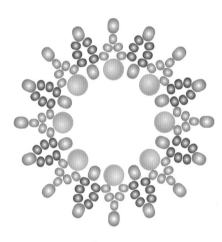

figure 5

Flower 4

Flower 3

Flower 5

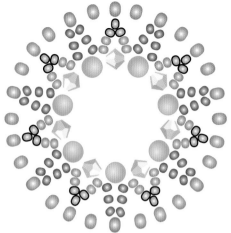

figure 6

Flower 5

See figure 6. String one 3-mm bicone and one 3-mm pearl; repeat six more times for a total of 14 beads on the thread. Pass through the first bead strung to make a ring, then weave again through all the beads to secure the thread. End with the thread exiting a pearl.

*String six green 15°s and pass again through the pearl to form an arc, then pass through the next bicone. String four golden 15°s and pass again through the bicone to form an arc, then pass through the pearl. Repeat from * six more times as you bead your way around the entire ring. At the end the thread should exit the third of the six 15° seed beads in the first arc.

**Pick up one bronze 11°, then weave forward to the middle of the next golden arc. Add three golden 15°s, then weave forward to the middle of the next green arc. Repeat from ** six more times as you bead your way around the ring. End with the thread exiting the first bronze 11° added in this row.

String three golden 11°s, skip the arc of 15°s, and pass through the 11° in the next arc. Repeat six more times. Place one 14-mm rivoli upside-down into the bezel you've formed, pull the thread, and weave twice more through this row of beads to secure the thread. End with the thread exiting the second of the three golden 11° seed beads first added. Pick up one golden 11° and pass through the second 11° seed bead in the next group of three. Repeat six more times to work completely around the ring. Weave twice more through this row of beads to secure the thread.

▶ Links

The long links are made in RAW and have either a 3-mm bicone or a 3-mm pearl in the center. Every second fringe ends with a short link—this is important to the placement of the flowers. Short links are made with only two units of RAW, without the center bead (bicone or pearl).

The links start and end with an 11° seed bead on the back of one flower or at the choker. For the first unit, string one

green 15°, one golden 11°, and one green 15°, and pass again through the 11° bead from which the thread exited, then weave forward so the thread exits the golden 11° just added. Repeat the same bead count for the next unit. For a long link, add a center unit as follows: String one 15°, one 11°, one 3-mm bicone, one 11°, and one 15°. Pass again through the bead from which the thread originally exited, then weave forward so the thread exits the bicone. Complete the other half of the long link by mirroring the first half (figure 7).

You can create a variation of this link using a pearl instead of a bicone, and green 15° seed beads in the center.

To complete the link, embellish the outer edges by weaving through the beads and adding one bronze 11° seed bead in each gap (figure 8).

figure 7

figure 8

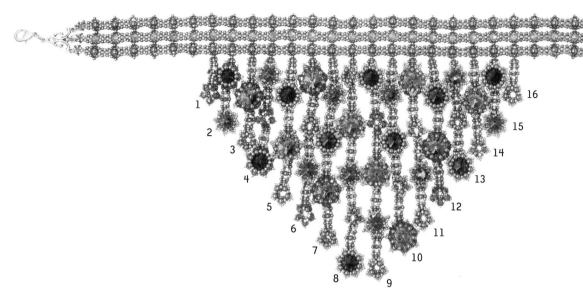

▶ Assemble

You'll build 16 fringes that are attached to bronze 11° beads in the arcs below the 16 pearls in the middle of the lower strand of the choker. The beading starts at the bottom end of each fringe and works up to the connection with the choker band. The sample shown uses 10 Flower 1s, eight Flower 2s, 10 Flower 3s, 10 Flower 4s, and 10 Flower 5s, attached with links as follows.

Fringes from Left to Right

1: Flower 1, long link with pearl.

2: Flower 3, long link with bicone, Flower 4, short link.

3: Flower 2, long link with pearl, Flower 5, long link with bicone.

4: Flower 4, long link with a bicone, Flower 1, long link with pearl, Flower 3, short link.

5: Flower 1, long link with pearl, Flower 5, long link with bicone, Flower 4, long link with pearl.

6: Flower 1, long link with pearl, Flower 3, long link with bicone, Flower 2, long link with pearl, Flower 5, short link.

7: Flower 2, long link with pearl, Flower 5, long link with bicone, Flower 4, long link with pearl, Flower 3, long link with bicone.

8: Flower 4, long link with pearl, Flower 1, long link with bicone, Flower 3, long link with pearl, Flower 5, long link with bicone, Flower 2, short link.

9: Flower 2, long link with bicone, Flower 3, long link with pearl, Flower 5, long link with bicone, Flower 1, long link with pearl, Flower 4, short link.

10: Flower 5, long link with bicone, Flower 1, long link with pearl, Flower 4, long link with bicone, Flower 3, long link with pearl.

11: Flower 2, long link with pearl, Flower 3, long link with bicone, Flower 1, long link with pearl, Flower 5, short link.

12: Flower 1, long link with bicone, Flower 5, long link with pearl, Flower 4, long link with bicone.

13: Flower 4, long link with pearl, Flower 2, long link with bicone, Flower 3, short link.

14: Flower 1, long link with bicone, Flower 5, long link with pearl.

15: Flower 3, long link with pearl, Flower 4, short link.

16: Flower 2, long link with bicone.

Attach an endpiece to each end of the choker, using 5-mm jump rings to connect the beaded loops to the loops of the endpiece. Attach the lobster clasp to one endpiece with a 6-mm jump ring. Attach the chain to the other endpiece with a 6-mm jump ring. Add one 5-mm jump ring to the other end of the chain and the remaining two 5-mm jump rings evenly spaced along the chain—these will allow you to adjust the length of the choker. Add the small pendant to the 5-mm jump ring at the end of the chain.

SUPPLIES

Size 11° metallic purple
cylinder beads, 1 g

Size 11° galvanized eggplant
seed beads, 2 g

28 size 8° gunmetal amethyst
seed beads

Size 15° galvanized silver
seed beads, 1 g

14 violet AB crystal bicones, 3 mm

2 violet rivolis, 18 mm

2 silver ear wires

FireLine, smoke, 6-pound test

Size 12 beading needle

Small sharp scissors

2 pairs of flat-nose pliers

FINISHED SIZE

1⅛ inches (28 mm) in diameter

SWEET EIGHTEEN EARRINGS

These earrings got their name quite simply: The rivoli at the center
has a diameter of 18 millimeters. Fringes of little bicones
in front highlight its sparkle.

1 String five cylinder beads and one size 11° seed bead; repeat six more times, for a total of 42 beads on your thread. Pass through the first bead strung to form the base ring. Weave through all the beads twice more, ending with the thread exiting the fourth of the first five cylinder beads strung.

2 String one 8°, one 11°, and one 8°; skip three beads in the base ring (one cylinder, one 11°, and one cylinder) and weave through the next three cylinder beads. Repeat six more times, until you've worked all around the ring. Pass through the first 8° added in this row.

3 *String three 11°s and pass through the next 8°. String one cylinder bead, two 15°s, one cylinder bead, and pass through the next 8°. Repeat from * until you've worked all the way around the ring. Weave forward to pass through the first 15° added in this row, and end with the thread heading toward the middle of the ring (figure 1).

4 Refer to figure 2 as you work this step. String one bicone and three 15°s; pass back through the bicone and then weave through the next 15° and cylinder (*not*

the ones from which the thread exited— you're beading in a zigzag along the ring). Weave forward through the 8° and the next 11°, then string five 15°s, skip the 11° in the middle, and weave through the next 11° and 8° seed beads. Weave through the next cylinder and 15° toward the middle of the ring and add another fringe of bicones.

Repeat until the ring is finished. End with the thread exiting a size 11° seed bead (one added in the second row, between the two size 8° seed beads). The thread should be heading toward the back of the beadwork. Turn the piece over.

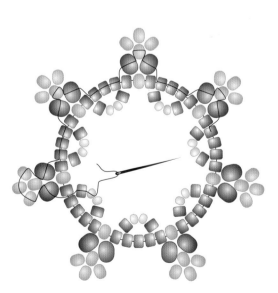

figure 1

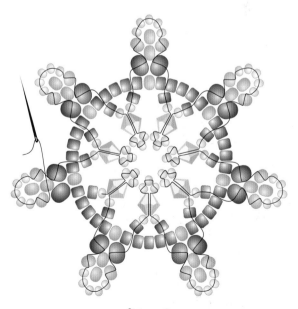

figure 2

5 Refer to figure 3 for steps 5 through 8. String five 11°s and pass through the corresponding size 11° seed bead in the next picot (shown with a black outline in figure 3). Continue in this manner until you've beaded seven arcs along the ring. Pass through the first three 11°s added in first arc.

6 Place the rivoli in the ring with the back facing you. String four cylinder beads and weave through the third 11° in the next arc. Repeat six more times to bead completely around the ring. At the end, weave forward and exit the third cylinder bead in the first group of four.

7 String two cylinder beads and weave through the second and third cylinder beads in the next group of four (the new beads are outlined in green in figure 3). Repeat six more times to bead around the ring; at the end, pass through the first pair of cylinder beads added in this row. Pick up one 11° and pass through the next pair of cylinder beads added in this row. Repeat six more times to complete the ring. Weave several times through the cylinders and 11°s added in this step to secure the thread.

Starting from the 11° marked with a red dot in figure 3, make a loop of five 11° beads; pass through the loop again, adding 15°s in the gaps between the 11°s. Weave through the loop once more and attach an ear wire to this loop.

Repeat all steps to make a second earring.

figure 3

Alternate Colorway

SABINE LIPPERT'S BEADED FANTASIES

SUPPLIES

1 heliotrope rivoli, 18 mm

5 rose satin chatons, 8 mm

Size 11° light bronze cylinder beads, 2 g

Size 11° galvanized champagne-colored seed beads, 2 g

Size 15° galvanized light gold seed beads, 2 g

30 blue-violet 2XAB crystal bicones, 3 mm

5 red AB satin crystal bicones, 4 mm

5 bronze glass pearls, 6 mm

1 golden jump ring, 6 mm

FireLine, 6-pound test

Size 12 beading needle

Small sharp scissors

2 pairs of flat-nose pliers

FINISHED SIZE

1¾ inches (4.4 cm) in diameter

AMAZON JEWEL PENDANT

I called the first version of this pendant Rainforest because it was emerald green (you can see it on page 73). I felt it needed some improvement, so it evolved into the piece you see here. I like to think that this pendant looks like something a conquistador's wife might have lost in the Amazon jungle.

Note: The pendant is made in three steps. First you'll bezel the rivoli. Then you'll bezel the five chatons and attach them to the last row of the bezeled rivoli. As a last step, you'll fill and embellish the gaps between the chatons.

▶ Bezel the Rivoli

1 Refer to figure 1 as you work steps 1 through 6. String three cylinder beads and one 11° seed bead; repeat nine times, for a total of 40 beads on your thread. Pass through the first bead strung to create a ring, then weave again through all the beads. End with the thread exiting a cylinder in front of an 11° seed bead.

2 Pick up one 11° seed bead and weave through the next three cylinder beads. Repeat nine more times to complete this row of the ring. Weave forward so the thread exits a cylinder bead in front of a pair of 11°s.

3 String three 15°s, skip the pair of 11°s, and weave through the next three cylinder beads. Repeat nine more times as you bead around the ring. The three 15° seed beads form little picots that push the 11° seed beads in the first row toward the middle of the ring. The thread exits a size 11° seed bead at the outside.

4 String one 15°, two cylinders, and one 15°; pass through the next 11° in the ring. Repeat nine times as you bead around the ring. (These beads are outlined in black in figure 1.) At the end, weave forward so the thread exits a 15° in front of an 11° seed bead.

5 Pick up one 11° and weave through the next group of four beads (a 15°, two cylinders, and a 15°). Repeat nine more times, beading your way around the ring. (These beads are outlined in red in figure 1.) Weave forward so the thread exits the first 11° added in this row.

6 For the last row, string three cylinder beads and weave through the next 11° in the previous row. Repeat nine more times. Loosen the thread and place the rivoli face down into the cup you've formed. Weave several times through the beads of the last row to secure the thread. Then weave back to the beads of the fourth row so the thread exits the group of four beads (a 15°, two cylinder beads, and a 15°).

7 Pick up one 11° seed bead and weave through the next four beads (a 15°, two cylinder beads, and a 15°). Repeat nine more times to bead completely around the ring. (These beads are outlined in black in figure 2.) End with the thread exiting the first 11° added in this row.

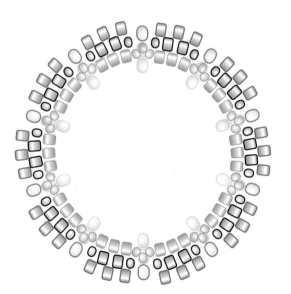

figure 1

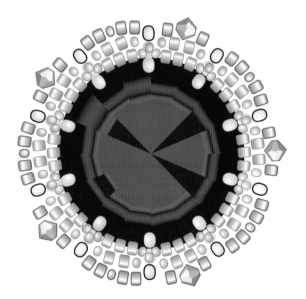

figure 2

8 Still referring to figure 2, string two cylinder beads, one 15°, and two more cylinders; pass through the next 11°. Pick up one cylinder bead, one 3-mm bicone, and one cylinder; pass through the next 11°. Repeat this sequence four more times until the ring is complete. Secure the thread and cut it off.

▶ Bezel the Chatons

The chaton bezel has a short side on the top, two sides (left and right) of medium length, and one long side on the bottom. The units will be attached with the short side adjacent to the rivoli bezel.

1 Refer to figure 3 for steps 1 through 6. For the first row, string three cylinders, one 11°, four cylinders, one 11°, five cylinders, one 11°, four cylinders, and one 11°. Pass through the first bead strung to make a ring, then weave again through all the beads. End with the thread exiting a cylinder bead in front of an 11°.

2 Pick up one 11° and weave through the next cylinder beads. Repeat three more times. At the end weave forward so the thread exits a cylinder bead in front of a pair of 11°s.

3 String three 15°s and weave through the next cylinder beads. Repeat three more times. End with the thread exiting an 11° seed bead added in step 2, heading toward the outside of the square.

4 For the next row, add one 15°, two cylinders, and one 15° to the short side, then pass through the next size 11° seed bead. For the medium-length sides, add five cylinders; and on the long side, add two cylinders, one 11°, and two cylinders. These beads are outlined in black in figure 3.

Reverse side

5 In the next row, add one 11° seed bead at each corner. These beads are outlined in red in figure 3.

6 In the last row, add one cylinder to the short side, two cylinders to the medium sides, and three cylinders to the long side. These beads are outlined in green in figure 3. Loosen the thread and place a chaton into the cup you've formed, upside-down. Pull the thread and weave several times through the last row of beads to secure the thread.

figure 3

7 Weave back to the beads in the fourth row and add one 11° at each of the corners, weaving through the beads in the fourth row to get from corner to corner. The thread exits an 11° seed bead added in this row.

8 To fill the gaps between these four 11° corner beads, on the medium sides add one 15°, one cylinder, one 3-mm bicone, one cylinder bead, and one 15°. On the long side, add two 11°s, one 3-mm bicone, and two 11°s. On the short side, weave through the beads of the bezeled rivoli as described on the next page. Each bezeled chaton is attached to the large rivoli in this last row.

Repeat steps 1 through 8 to bezel four more chatons.

▶ Attach the Chatons to the Rivoli

This step describes how to attach all of the chatons to the central gem (two are shown attached in figure 4). The short side is the one used to attach the bezeled chaton to the bezeled rivoli. Exiting from the 11° seed bead at the beginning of the short side, weave through the group of five beads (consisting of two cylinder beads, one 15°, and two cylinder beads) in the last row of the bezeled rivoli (these beads are outlined in red in figure 4). Then pass through the 11° seed bead at the end of the short side of the bezeled chaton. Secure the thread by weaving twice through the beads in this last row.

▶ Add the Embellishments

1 After adding the fifth chaton, fill the gaps between the chatons as follows. To build the little fringes, weave through the line of beads used to attach the chatons so the thread exits the 11° belonging to the chaton bezel, at the end of the attachment (these beads are outlined in black in figure 5). String three 15°s, one 11°, one 4-mm bicone, and three 15°s; weave back through the bicone and the 11°. String three 15°s and weave through the corresponding beads in the next chaton (the added beads are outlined in red in figure 5). Repeat four more times. Weave through the beadwork so the thread exits the group of five beads (consisting of two 11°s, one bicone, and two 11°s) on the long side of one bezeled chaton.

2 *String one 15°, one 11°, one 3-mm bicone, one 6-mm pearl, one 3-mm bicone, one 11°, and one 15°. Weave through the first two 11° beads in the last row of the long side of the chaton bezel so the thread exits in front of a bicone. String four 15°s, skip the bicone, and weave through the next two 11°s. Repeat from * four more times until the row is finished. The beads added in this row are outlined in red in figure 6. At the end, weave forward so the thread exits in front of a pearl.

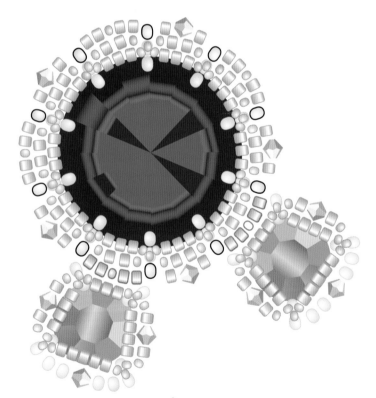

figure 4

3 Still referring to figure 6, *string eight 15°s, skip the pearl, and weave through the next beads until you reach the middle of the group of four 15° seed beads on top of the bicone. Pick up one 15° and weave through the beadwork until you reach the next pearl. Repeat from * four more times until the circle is finished. The beads in this row are outlined in green in the drawing.

At the end add a loop of five 11° seed beads to the size 15° seed bead in the middle of the beads above a bicone. Pass through the loop again, adding one 15° in each of the four gaps between the 11°s. Place a jump ring through the loop and string a chain or ribbon through the ring to wear the pendant.

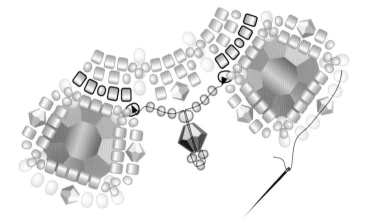

figure 5

Alternate Colorway

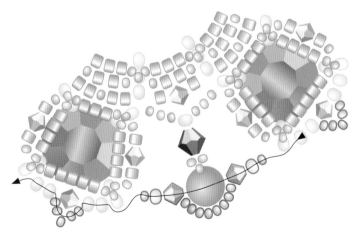

figure 6

SUPPLIES

3-mm dark brown bugle beads, 1 g

Size 11° galvanized golden seed beads, 1 g

Size 15° dark copper seed beads, 2 g

4 light peach 2XAB crystal chatons, 8 mm

20 yellow-orange crystal bicones, 4 mm

10 palest orange 2XAB crystal bicones, 3 mm

2 golden ear wires

FireLine, 6-pound test

Size 12 beading needle

Small sharp scissors

2 pairs of flat-nose pliers

FINISHED SIZE

1 inch (2.5 cm) long, not including ear wires

74

DOUBLE STAR EARRINGS

These earrings show a simple way to build a miniature sphere from a bezeled piece. Make two five-corner stars, placed them back to back, and join them. Of course, you could make a bunch of spheres and combine them to make a necklace or a bracelet.

1 Refer to figure 1 for steps 1 through 3. String one bugle bead and one 11° seed bead; repeat four more times for a total of 10 beads on your thread. Pass through the first bead strung to create a ring. Weave through the entire ring to secure the thread. End with the thread exiting a bugle bead.

2 Pick up one 11° seed bead and pass through the next bugle bead. Repeat four more times as you bead around the entire ring. End with the thread exiting a bugle bead.

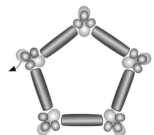

figure 1

3 String three 15° seed beads and weave through the next bugle bead. These three beads form a little picot at the gap between the two 11°s. Repeat four more times to bead around the ring. End with the thread exiting an 11° seed bead at the outside of this ring, which was added in step 2.

4 String one 15°, one bugle bead, and one 15°; pass through the next 11°. Repeat four more times to bead around the entire ring. These beads are outlined in red in figure 2. End with the thread exiting a 15° seed bead in front of an 11° seed bead.

5 Pick up one 11° (outlined in green in figure 2) and weave through the next 15°, the next bugle bead, and the next 15°. Repeat four more times to bead around the ring. Pass through the first 11° added in this round.

6 Pick up one bugle bead (outlined in blue in figure 2) and pass through the next 11° seed bead from the previous step. Repeat four more times as you weave around the ring. Weave forward through the first bugle bead in this row. Pull the thread to tighten the ring, then loosen it again and place the chaton into the bezel from the

back, with the chaton facing upside-down. Pull the thread again and, with high thread tension, weave through the beads in the last round until it is secure. Weave back to the beads in the fourth row (15°, bugle, 15°), and end with the thread exiting a 15° seed bead in front of an 11° seed bead.

7 Refer to figure 3 as you work steps 7 and 8. String three 15°s (outlined in red in figure 3) and weave through the next 15°, bugle, and 15°. Repeat four more times as you bead around the ring. These beads, together with the 15°s in the fourth row, form a group of five 15°s. Weave forward so the thread exits the second 15° in the first group of three added in this row.

8 String two 15°s, one 4-mm bicone, and two 15°s (outlined in green in figure 3), and pass through the middle 15° in the next group of three. Repeat four more times to complete the ring. End with the thread exiting in front of the first added bicone.

9 String six 15°s (outlined in red in figure 4), skip the bicone, weave through the next two 15°s, skip the next 15°, and weave through the two 15°s in front of the next bicone. Repeat four more times to complete the circle. Weave forward so the thread exits the third 15°—in the middle—in the first group of six.

10 Pick up one 11° and weave through the next three 15°s. String one 15°, one 3-mm bicone, and one 15°, and weave through the first three 15°s in the next group of six above the 4-mm bicone. The new beads in this row are outlined in green in figure 4. Repeat this step four more times as you bead around the ring, then secure the thread and cut it off.

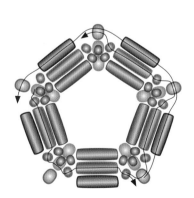

figure 2

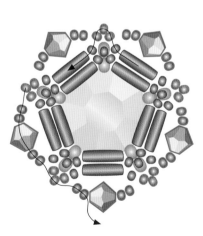

figure 3

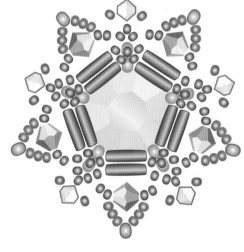

figure 4

11 Repeat steps 1 through 9 to bead another star shape. The last row of this component will be connected to the last row of the previous component you made, with the components back to back. So for this row you don't add 11°s or 3-mm bicones, but instead weave through the corresponding 11°s and bicones of the previous star, adding only the 15°s in front of and after the 3-mm bicones (figure 5).

12 After connecting the stars, bead a loop using seven size 15° seed beads, starting from one 11° seed bead above a bicone. Weave through the loop again, adding one 15° in each of the four gaps, then weave through all beads again to strengthen. Attach an ear wire to the loop.

Repeat all steps to make a second earring.

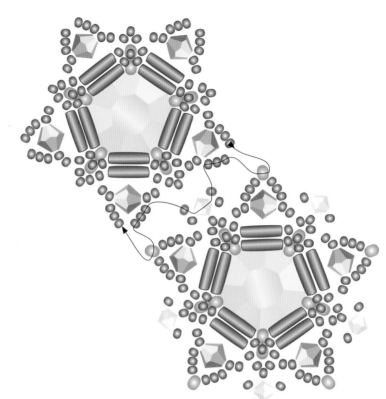

figure 5

Alternate Colorway

SABINE LIPPERT'S BEADED FANTASIES

MILADY PENDANT

This amulet combines hexagonal bezeled rivolis and 8-mm round beads bezeled in a square shape. These two kinds of units are then combined into a larger square shape with an embellished center. It's reminiscent of a bijoux worn spectacularly by Faye Dunaway as Milady in *The Three Musketeers*.

SUPPLIES

Size 11° galvanized
reddish-brown seed beads, 3 g

Size 11° light bronze
cylinder beads, 3 g

Size 15° light bronze seed beads, 2 g

4 topaz rivolis, 14 mm

44 bronze glass pearls, 3 mm

32 bronze 2X crystal bicones, 3 mm

8 dark green glass pearls, 8 mm

1 bronze jump ring

FireLine, smoke, 6-pound test

Size 12 beading needle

Small sharp scissors

2 pairs of flat-nose pliers

FINISHED SIZE

2 inches (5.1 cm) square

You'll make a series of alternating bezeled rivolis and pearls that share some of the beads in their last rows, which attaches these components to each other.

1 Refer to figure 1 for steps 1 through 3. String one size 11° seed bead, one cylinder bead, one 3-mm pearl, and one cylinder bead. Repeat this sequence five more times for a total of 24 beads on your thread. Pass through the first bead strung to form a ring, then weave again through all the beads to secure. End with the thread exiting a cylinder in front of an 11°. This forms the base ring.

2 String one 11°, skip the 11° of the base ring, and weave through the next three beads (cylinder, pearl, cylinder). Repeat five more times to complete the row. End with the thread exiting a cylinder in front of a pair of 11°s. String three 15°s, skip the pair of 11°s, and weave through the next three beads (cylinder, pearl, cylinder). Repeat five more times to complete the row. End with the thread exiting an 11° at the outside of the ring. String two cylinders, one 11°, and two cylinders, and pass through the next 11° at the outside of the ring. Repeat five more times. Weave forward and pass through the first 11° added in this row.

3 The next two rows are netting rows that secure the rivoli. For the first row, string five cylinder beads and pass through the next 11° added in the previous row. Repeat five more times. End with the thread exiting the third of five cylinder beads added in this row. Place the rivoli into the vessel, upside-down. String three cylinder beads and pass through the middle cylinder bead in the next group of five. Repeat five more times, then weave twice more through the beads in this row to secure the bezel.

4 To build the lower side of the bezel and form the attaching points, weave through the beadwork to exit an 11° in the fourth row. You'll add two different sequences of beads between the 11°s in the fourth row. For sequence 1, string two cylinders, one 11°, and two cylinders, then pass through the next 11°. For sequence 2, string one 15°, one 11°, one bicone, one 11°, and one 15°, then pass through the next 11°. Repeat sequence 2 twice more, work sequence 1, then work sequence 2 again. The components will be attached at the sequence 1 positions (figure 2).

5 String one 8-mm pearl, four cylinders, one 11°, and four cylinders; pass through the 8-mm pearl again to form a half-circle, then weave through all the beads again

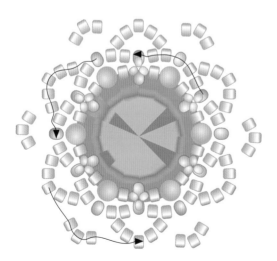

figure 1

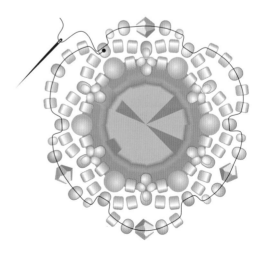

figure 2

to secure the ring, exiting from the 8-mm pearl. String four cylinders, one 11°, and four cylinders; pass through the 8-mm pearl. Weave through all the beads again to secure the ring, then pass through the last added bead. The thread exits a cylinder bead in front of the hole of the 8-mm pearl. Pick up one 11° and weave along a half-circle of beads to the next gap, add another 11°, and weave forward through the next four cylinders (figure 3).

6 Pick up one 11° and weave through the next four cylinder beads. Repeat three more times. End with the thread exiting a cylinder in front of an 11° added in this row. String three 15°s and weave through the next four cylinders. Repeat three more times. End with the thread exiting an 11° added in the previous row. Add four cylinder beads in the gaps between the size 11° seed beads, then weave another time through the beads in this row. This is the back side of the bezeled round. Now weave forward through the beads so that the thread exits an 11° on the front side.

7 String two 15°s, one 3-mm pearl, and two 15°s, and pass through the next 11°. Repeat three times. Weave again through the beads just added to secure the thread, then weave forward so the thread exits a group of three 15°s.

8 The following row has two bead sequences. For sequence 1, string two cylinders, one 11°, and two cylinders; weave through the next set of three 15°s. For sequence 2, string one 15°, one 11°, one bicone, one 11°, and one 15°; weave through the next set of three 15°s (figure 4).

The components will be attached as shown in figure 5. For the next sequence 1, don't add beads but weave through two cylinders, one 11°, and two cylinders of a bezeled

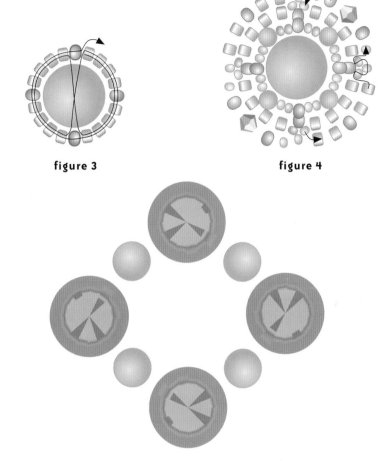

figure 3

figure 4

figure 5

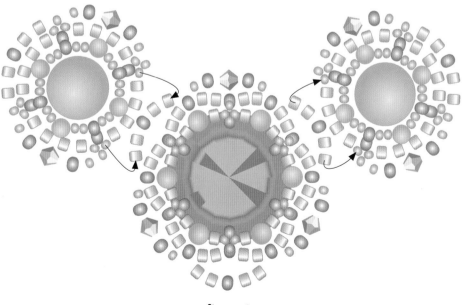

figure 6

Reverse side

rivoli to attach the components. Add another sequence 2. Figure 6 shows how the components are attached.

9 After attaching all eight units, weave along the outer rim, through the rows with two sequences, and add 15°s in the gaps between the units to stiffen the piece. Weave to the middle so the thread exits an 11° next to a bicone for one of the bezeled pearls.

10 String one 15°, one 11°, one bicone, one 3-mm pearl, one bicone, one 11°, and one 15°; weave through the 11°, bicone, and 11° in the next bezeled pearl. Beads added are outlined in black in figure 7. Repeat three more times to complete the circle. End with the thread exiting a bicone in front of a 3-mm pearl. String one 15°, one 11°, and one 15°, skip the pearl, and weave through the next beads, exiting in front of the next 3-mm pearl. Repeat three more times, then exit the first 11° added in this step. The beads added in this step are outlined in red in figure 7. String one 15°, one 11°, one 8-mm pearl, one 11°, and one 15°; pass through the next 11° added in the

previous row. Beads added in this step are outlined in green in figure 7. Repeat three more times. End with the thread exiting an 8-mm pearl.

11 Push the center unit just added toward the back and continue beading from the back side. Add two 15°s between each of the 8-mm pearls. Weave through the beads again and add one 15° between each of the two 15°s just added. Weave back to the first row added in the center so the thread exits in front of a 3-mm pearl. String three 15° seed beads above the 8-mm pearl and weave through the next beads. Repeat three more times. Make sure you have really good tension on the thread—the function of this last step is to push the round beads a bit to the outside, so they are secured above the bicones of the rivoli. This gives stability to the entire piece.

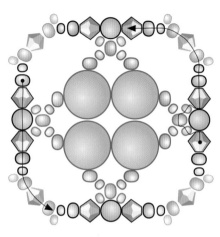

figure 7

12 To hang the amulet, you can add a loop on the outside, starting from a bicone in a round unit. Or you can add loops at two of the corners, so the amulet doesn't twist when you wear it on a long chain.

Alternate Colorway

CHAPTER 4
A QUESTION OF ARCHITECTURE

How do you prevent a beaded structure from collapsing when there's nothing to fill its center? How do you stabilize a piece so it's sturdy enough to keep its shape? Which changes transform a piece from a ring to a bangle to a square? It's just a matter of structural design.

SUPPLIES

56 jet black 2XAB crystal bicones, 3 mm

Size 11° dark bronze seed beads, 1 g

Size 15° dark bronze seed beads, 3 g

Size 11° copper cylinder beads, 2 g

40 champagne-colored glass pearls, 3 mm

2 jet black 2XAB bicones, 4 mm

2 copper head pins

2 copper ear wires

FireLine, 6-pound test

Size 12 beading needle

Small sharp scissors

Round-nose pliers

Flat-nose pliers

FINISHED SIZE

2¼ inches (5.7 cm), not including ear wires

82

CHER'S EARRINGS

I was given a challenge to make some really extravagant earrings, something like what Cher might wear onstage. I thought I'd better keep adding more flowers! It's important, when creating earrings, to embellish the back side, too. So the floral elements have twinkling bicones on the front and elegant glass pearls on the back.

1 String one 3-mm bicone and one 11° seed bead; repeat this sequence four more times for a total of 10 beads on your thread. Pass through the first bead strung to create a ring, then weave twice through the ring. End with the thread exiting an 11° bead.

2 Figure 1 shows this step and the next. String four 15°s and pass through the 11° bead again, forming a small arc. Weave forward through the next bicone. String four 15°s and pass through the bicone again, forming an arc above the bicone, then pass through the next 11°. Repeat four more times, beading around the entire ring. At the end, weave forward so the thread exits between the second and third 15° in the first arc—the one at the size 11° seed bead.

3 Pick up one cylinder bead and weave through the next four 15°s. Pick up one 15° and again weave through the next four 15°s. Repeat four more times until the ring is finished, always using a cylinder bead at the arcs above the 11° seed beads, and a 15° seed bead at the arcs above the bicones. End with the thread exiting a cylinder bead.

4 Pick up one crystal pearl and weave through the next cylinder bead. Repeat four more times, then weave again through the beads in the last ring at least twice; the thread should be secured and exiting a cylinder bead (figure 2).

5 You'll bead the stalks of the little flowers in four different lengths. Later, when you connect them, it'll be important to start with the shortest and end with the longest, in the ring. To explain the construction of the stalk, figure 3 shows the second longest one.

Starting from the cylinder bead on the back side of the flower, build three units of RAW—the first and the third bead of each unit are 15°s, and the second one is a cylinder bead. For the next unit—the center unit—string one 15°, one 11°, one 3-mm bicone, one 11°, and one 15°; pass again through the cylinder bead from which the thread exited. Weave forward so the thread exits the bicone. String one 11°, one 15°, one cylinder bead, one 15°, and one 11°; pass again through the bicone, then weave forward so the thread exits the cylinder bead. Now make another three units of RAW the same as at the beginning of the stalk.

6 Here's a simple trick to tidy up the single row of RAW beads, which doesn't look very neat at this point. Simply weave through the beads in the row in the following way: With the thread exiting from right to left, stitch one bead down, then go right, then go down one, then go left, etc. Complete the number of turns necessary through the RAW units on one side of the bicone unit so they're even on both sides. Once you've done this, weave back from the end of the stalk to the bicone. Weave through the beads around the bicone of this unit and add one 11° between the two 11°s on the left and one 11° between the two 11°s on the right. Then complete the beading to tidy up the other half of the stalk (figure 4).

figure 1

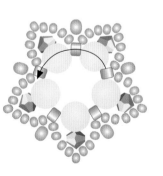

figure 2

figure 3

figure 4

7 Bead a total of four stalks: The smallest has one RAW unit in front of and after the center unit; the second one (described in step 5) has three RAW units in front of and after the center unit; the third stalk has five units; and the fourth stalk has seven units in front of and after the center unit.

8 After finishing the fourth flower with the stalk, your thread should exit the cylinder bead on top of the stalk. Weave through the cylinder beads on top of the other stalks and make a ring with these four beads. Take care to keep the units in the right sequence (from shortest to longest). Weave twice through the beads in this ring, then add one 11° between each of the four cylinder beads. End with the thread exiting an 11° seed bead (figure 5).

9 Figure 6 illustrates this step and the next one. String one 15°, one 11°, and one 15°; pass through the next 11°. Repeat three more times. At the end, the thread exits the first 11° added in this step.

10 Pick up one 15°, one 3-mm bicone, and one 15°; pass through the next 11° that was added in the previous step. Repeat three more times to work completely around the ring, then secure the thread and cut it off.

Repeat steps 1 through 10 to make a second component.

To mount each component to an ear wire, thread a head pin through the center of the top ring, pick up one 4-mm bicone, and then make a loop with the end of the head pin. Attach the ear wire to the loop.

figure 5

figure 6

SUPPLIES

42 bronze fire-polished
beads, 4 mm

36 aquamarine-blue
fire-polished beads, 3 mm

14 bronze round beads, 6 mm

Size 11° transparent blue-violet
seed beads, 2 g

Size 15° light gold seed beads, 3 g

2 golden jump rings, 5 mm

2 golden ear wires

FireLine, 8-pound test

Size 12 beading needle

Small sharp scissors

2 pairs of flat-nose pliers

FINISHED SIZE

2 inches (5.1 cm),
not including ear wires

I CAN'T DANCE
EARRINGS

I often have a little story about how I named a piece. When I finished these
earrings and showed a picture of them to a friend, she asked me, "Are they heavy?"
"No, quite comfortable, but I wouldn't dance all night wearing them!" They're built
with a base of right angle weave using beads in three different sizes,
then covered with a net of 15° seed beads.

1 You'll build six units in RAW, using 6-mm rounds on one side, 3-mm fire-polished beads on the opposite side, and 4-mm fire-polished beads for the middle (horizontal) beads. Work as follows: For the first unit, string one 4-mm fire-polished bead, one 6-mm round, one 4-mm fire-polished bead, and one 3-mm fire-polished bead. Make a ring by passing through the first bead strung, and weave a second time through the ring to secure the thread, which should exit a 4-mm fire-polished bead in front of a 3-mm fire-polished bead. For the second unit, string one 3-mm fire-polished bead, one 4-mm fire-polished bead, and one 6-mm round bead; weave through the 4-mm fire-polished bead originally exited, then through the 3-mm and 4-mm fire-polished beads just added. Continue in this manner, adding RAW units in alternating clockwise/counterclockwise directions, until you have six complete units. Due to the different bead sizes, the beadwork starts to curve and you can close it into a ring with the seventh unit. To do so, pick up a 6-mm round bead at the outside, weave through the 4-mm fire-polished bead in the first square, and add a 3-mm fire-polished bead at the inside (figure 1 shows this step and the next).

2 Weave to the outside of the ring so the thread exits a 6-mm round bead. Bead seven RAW units on the back side in the same way as the front, incorporating the 6-mm rounds from the front into the new RAW units. The fire-polished beads will be in two layers when the second ring is complete.

3 In this step, you'll fill the gaps at the crossing points between the beads. Filling these gaps has two aims: The beads cover the thread, and they serve as attachment beads for the netting. With the thread exiting a 3-mm fire-polished bead in the inner circle on the back side, pick up one 11° and weave through the next 3-mm fire-polished bead. Repeat six more times to complete the ring, then weave to the outside and pass through a 6-mm round. Pick up one 4-mm fire-polished bead and pass through the next round bead (figure 2). Repeat six more times, then weave to the center of the ring on the other side, and fill the gaps between the 3-mm fire-polished beads with size 11° seed beads.

4 Now you'll bead the top layer of netting. With the thread exiting a size 11° seed bead in the inner ring of one side, string three 15°s, one 11°, and three 15°s; pass through the next 11° in the ring, creating an arc shape. Make a total of seven arcs, working around the ring. At the end, weave forward through the beads in the first arc so the thread exits the size 11° seed bead in the middle of the first arc (figure 3 shows steps 4 through 8).

5 For the next circle of arcs, string five 15°s, pass through the 4-mm fire-polished bead on the outside ring, string five more 15°s, and pass through the size 11° seed bead in the next arc. Repeat six more times until you've beaded around the entire ring. Weave forward so the thread exits a 4-mm fire-polished bead on the outside of the ring.

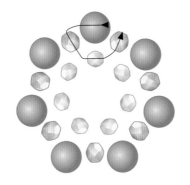

figure 1

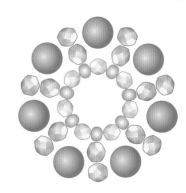

figure 2

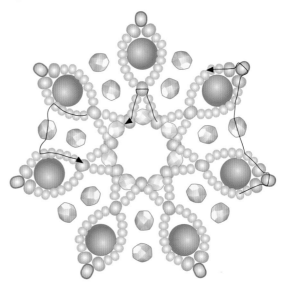

figure 3

and repeat the step there. Again weave forward to the opposite side so the thread exits in the middle of four 15° seed beads. Add one 11° in the middle, then weave through the next two 15°s and along the beads to the opposite side, where you should repeat the step. Secure the thread and cut it off.

Repeat steps 1 through 10 to make a second earring. To assemble the earrings, use a jump ring to connect the loop in the beadwork to the hole in the ear wire.

Alternate Colorway

6 Here you'll add embellishment on the outside of the ring. String two 15°s, two 11°s, and two 15°s; pass through the next 4-mm fire-polished bead, forming an arc. Repeat six more times as you work around the ring. At the end, weave forward through the first arc in this step so the thread exits between the two size 11° seed beads.

7 Pick up one 11° (outlined in red in figure 3) and weave through the following beads: one 11°, two 15°s, one 4-mm fire-polished bead, two 15°s, and one 11°. Repeat six more times as you work around the ring.

8 Next you'll build the netting on the back side. The easiest way is to start in the middle, with the thread exiting a size 11° seed bead. Bead the first and second circle of arcs as described in steps 4 and 5. **Note:** The third circle on the outside (steps 6 and 7) is *not* repeated.

9 Starting from one of the size 11° seed beads on the outside, make a small band of RAW units, as follows. String three 11°s for the first unit and pass through the 11°

originally exited and the first two beads just added. String one 11°, one 3-mm fire-polished bead, and one 11° for the second unit (the thread exits the fire-polished bead). For the third unit, string three 3-mm fire-polished beads (the thread exits the middle of these three beads). For the fourth and fifth units, in each case, pick up three 11°s (each time, the thread exits the second of these three beads). When you're done, make a loop of five size 11° seed beads. Weave twice through the six beads in the ring on top (figure 4).

10 To strengthen and embellish the band, add one size 15° in each of the four gaps between the size 11° seed beads in the loop. Be careful not to fill the gaps in front of and after the 11° seed bead that serves as the start of the loop. Then fill each of the four gaps on the left and each of the four gaps on the right side of the band with one 11° and one 15° in front of and after the 11° where you change to the opposite side (outlined in black in figure 5).

Weave forward so the thread exits an 11° seed bead just added in front of a fire-polished bead. String four 15°s (outlined in red in figure 5), skip the fire-polished bead, and pass through the next 11°. Weave through the beads to the opposite side

figure 4

figure 5

SUPPLIES

10 bronze round glass pearls, 8 mm

Size 11° light bronze seed beads, 3 g

9 almond-colored drop pearls,
11 x 8 mm

16 size 8° bronze seed beads

16 clear copper crystal
bicones, 3 mm

A few size 15° seed beads

6 copper head pins

2 bronze round glass pearls, 4 mm

1 light topaz crystal donut,
15–17 mm

1 brown bicone, 8 mm

1 light topaz bicone, 8 mm

1 copper drop bead, 11 x 8 mm

1 copper round bead, 12 mm

42 inches (107 cm) of 8-mm
copper chain

8 copper jump rings, 5 mm

FireLine, 6-pound test

Size 12 beading needle

Small sharp scissors

2 pairs of flat-nose pliers

Round-nose pliers

FINISHED SIZE

Cross, 2¾ x 2¼ inches
(7 x 5.7 cm), including loops

THREE
CROSSES
NECKLACE

Named as it is, this design might make
you search for a trio of crossed elements,
but what actually happened is I made
three different versions of the
pendant, and this one turned out
to be my favorite. As the saying goes,
"All good things come in threes!"

▶ Pendant

1 String one 8-mm pearl, two size 11° seed beads, one drop pearl (from the wide to the narrow end), two 11°s, one drop pearl (from narrow to wide), and two 11°s. Repeat three more times for a total of 36 beads on the thread. Pass through the first bead strung to create a ring, then weave through all the beads, exiting a size 11° seed bead right after a pearl.

2 String one 11°, one 8-mm pearl, and one 11°, skip the next six beads (one seed, one drop, two seeds, one drop, and one seed), and weave through the next three beads (one seed, one pearl, and one seed). Repeat three more times, working your way around the ring (these beads are outlined in red in figure 1). Pull the thread tightly; the round beads will create the inner ring while the drop pearls form the edges of the cross. Weave through the beadwork so the thread exits a pearl.

3 Refer to figure 2 as you work steps 3 through 5. Pick up one 8° and pass through the next pearl. Repeat seven more times, maintaining good tension on the thread to secure the inner ring. End with the thread exiting an 8° bead.

4 String six 11°s and pass through the next 8°, forming an arc. Repeat seven more times. Weave through the beadwork so the thread exits the third bead in the first arc.

5 Pick up one 11° (outlined in red in figure 2), weave through the next three 11°s, skip the 8°, and weave through the next three 11°s. Repeat seven more times.

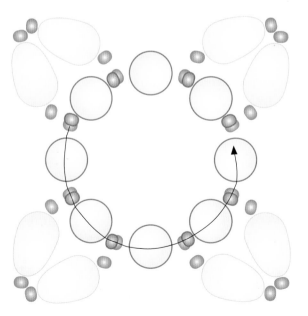

figure 1

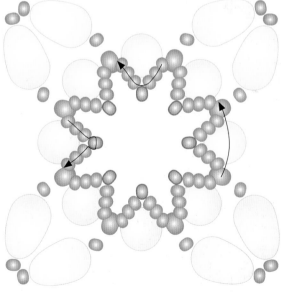

figure 2

Pass through the size 11° seed bead in the middle of the first arc.

6 Refer to figure 3 as you work steps 6 through 8. String one 11°, one bicone, and one 11°, and weave through the middle seed bead in the next arc. Repeat seven more times. Weave twice through this row of beads to secure the thread and stabilize the beads, then weave through the bead-work to one of the edges of the cross so the thread exits from the first 11° between two drop pearls.

7 Pick up one 11° and weave through the next three beads (seed bead, drop bead, seed bead). String eight 11°s, skip the round bead, and weave through the next three beads (seed bead, drop bead, seed bead). Repeat three more times. The added beads are outlined in red in figure 3. Weave through the beadwork to exit the fourth of eight 11° seed beads added in this row.

8 Pick up one 11° (outlined in green in figure 3) and weave through the next four 11°s. Repeat this on the three remaining sides.

9 Next, you'll add a loop to the top and to the bottom of the cross to hold the chain and embellishment. Begin with the thread exiting the middle 11° between two drops. String seven 11°s and pass through the 11° from which the thread exited. Weave twice through the beads forming the loop, then add one 15° between the second and third, third and fourth, fourth and fifth, and fifth and sixth 11°s to fill the gaps in the loop.

10 Repeat steps 3 through 6 on the other side of the pendant (beginning with adding 8°s between the pearls and ending with adding bicones at the inner circle).

▶ **Tassel Embellishment**

1 Make six drops as follows. For each one, place the beads described on a head pin, then form a loop at the top.

● One 4-mm pearl, one crystal donut, and one 4-mm pearl

● One 8-mm pearl and one brown bicone

● One 8-mm pearl and one topaz bicone

● One copper drop bead

● One copper round bead

● And ond one almond-colored drop pearl.

2 Cut a piece of chain 3 inches (7.6 cm) long. Using a jump ring, hang it from one of the pendant loops made in step 9. Attach one drop to each end of the chain. Attach the remaining four drops randomly—the tassel should not look "neat."

3 To wear the necklace, use a jump ring to attach the remaining chain to the loop on the other side of the pendant.

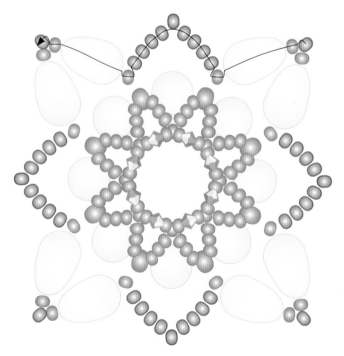

figure 3

SCHEHEREZADE PENDANT

I originally created a beaded bead in an oriental style and named it Scheherezade, after the narrator in *The Arabian Nights*. This ring-shaped pendant is based on that technique and therefore got the same name. It's probably my best-known design.

SUPPLIES

84 iris green fire-polished beads, 3 mm

56 iris green fire-polished beads, 4 mm

14 satin gold round beads, 6 mm

28 size 8° copper penny seed beads

Size 11° metallic gold iris seed beads, 3 g

Size 15° metallic gold iris seed beads, 3 g

FireLine, 6-pound test

Size 12 beading needle

Small sharp scissors

FINISHED SIZE

1¾ inches (4.4 cm) in diameter

Note: Bead the base with a rather low thread tension; because the piece will gain its stability from the netting in the last layer, you could have problems if the base is too stiff. Size 15° seed beads tend to vary in size, so you shouldn't automatically stick to the bead count described in these instructions. It may be necessary to add one more bead in the netting (especially at the outside).

1 Using 3-mm fire-polished beads, bead a strip of 13 units of RAW. Make one more unit of RAW, connecting it to the first unit to form the strip into a ring as follows: Pick up one 3-mm fire-polished bead, weave through the fire-polished bead at the other end of the strip, pick up one more 3-mm fire-polished bead, and weave again through the bead from which the thread exited. Weave again through the four beads in this last unit to stabilize the thread. Weave forward so the thread exits a side bead of the ring, which is the base ring.

2 Bead a second row of RAW as follows: String one 3-mm, one 4-mm, and one 3-mm fire-polished bead and pass again through the bead from which the thread exited. Weave forward so the thread exits the next 3-mm fire-polished bead in the base ring. String one 3-mm and one 4-mm fire-polished bead and weave through the 3-mm fire-polished bead of the previous unit and the one from which the thread exited for this unit. Weave forward so the thread exits the next 3-mm fire-polished bead in this unit (shown with an arrow in figure 1). Continue to weave units, alternating clockwise and counterclockwise directions, until you've added a second row to the entire ring; at the end, close the circle by joining the last unit to the first unit.

3 Weave forward so the thread exits a 4-mm fire-polished bead. **Note:** It does *not* matter at this point that the piece is soft and has little thread tension. For the first unit in the next row, string one 4-mm fire-polished bead, one 6-mm pearl, and one 4-mm fire-polished bead, and pass through the bead from which the thread exited. Repeat the RAW technique described in the previous step until you've beaded completely around the ring; finish the row by attaching the last unit to the first, adding only one 6-mm pearl here (figure 2).

4 Weave back to the base ring and repeat step 2 on the other side.

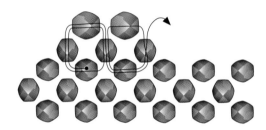

figure 1

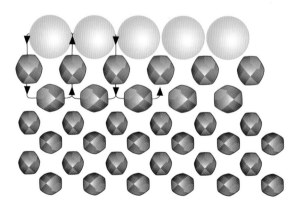

figure 2

5 The next row is a zipping row; use 4-mm fire-polished beads to complete RAW units connecting the 4-mm fire-polished bead in the previous step with the 6-mm pearls from step 3. This completes the base.

6 Weave back to the inner ring. Weave through the 3-mm fire-polished bead, adding one size 11° in each gap between the 3-mm fire-polished beads. Weave forward to the next row of 4-mm fire-polished beads and add one size 8° in each gap between the 4-mm fire-polished beads. Weave forward to the outside and add one 3-mm fire-polished bead in each gap between the 6-mm pearls (figure 3).

7 Weave forward to the other side of the base ring and repeat the second and first rows in step 6 to add 8°s in the gaps between the 4-mm fire-polished beads, and 11°s in the gaps between the 3-mm fire-polished beads in the inner ring. End with the thread exiting an 11° in this inner ring.

8 For the third layer, you'll weave four rows on each side of the ring to create a net. In the first and third rows you'll build arcs that are attached to the base in the second and fourth rows. Refer to figure 4 as you work the rest of the piece.

For the first row of arcs, string two 15°s, one 11°, and two 15°s, and pass through the next 11° in the base. Repeat thirteen more times to complete the ring. Weave forward so the thread exits the 11° in the middle of the first arc.

Now work an attachment row. String two 15°s, pass through the 8° bead on the base, string two 15°s, and pass through the 11° in the next arc. Repeat thirteen more times to finish the ring; end with the thread exiting a size 8° bead.

For the next row of arcs, string three 15°s, one 11°, and three 15°s, and pass through the next 8°. Repeat thirteen more times to bead around the whole ring, then weave forward so the thread exits the 11° in the first arc. The fourth row is another attachment row. String three 15°s (or four if the beads are very small), pass through the next 3-mm fire-polished bead, pick up another three (or four) 15°s, and pass through the 11° in the next arc. Repeat thirteen more times to bead around the entire ring, then add the same netting on the other side of the ring.

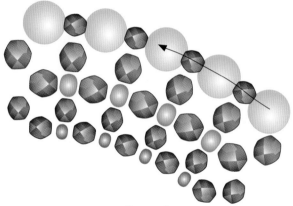

figure 3

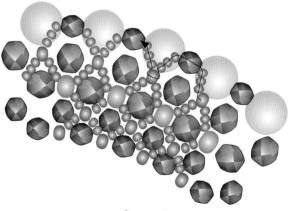

figure 4

Alternate Colorway

SUPPLIES

Size 11° bronze seed beads, 1 g

Size 15° golden seed beads, 1 g

48 antique brass crystal
pearls, 3 mm

28 antique brass crystal
pearls, 4 mm

12 yellow-orange crystal
bicones, 4 mm

2 hook eye pins

2 golden ear wires

6 small bell-shaped
pendants (for the tassels)

FireLine, 6-pound test

Size 12 beading needle

Small sharp scissors

Round-nose pliers

Flat-nose pliers

FINISHED SIZE

1 inch (2.5 cm) long,
not including ear wires or tassels

AISHA EARRINGS

I think my Aisha design looks very oriental. To create its oval shape,
I've played with different bead sizes in the RAW base. I then
covered it with a special kind of netting.

1 String six size 11° seed beads and pass through the first bead strung to create a ring. Weave through the beads again to secure.

2 String one 3-mm pearl, one 4-mm pearl, one bicone, one 4-mm pearl, and one 3-mm pearl, and pass again through the 11° from which the thread exited. *Pass through the next 11° in the ring and string one 3-mm pearl, one 4-mm pearl, and one bicone, and weave through the 4-mm pearl and the 3-mm pearl of the previous unit, then pass through the 11° again. Repeat from * three more times. Weave forward through the next 11°, and through the 3-mm and 4-mm pearls of the first step; add one bicone and weave through the 4-mm and 3-mm pearls of the previous unit. Weave forward so the thread exits a bicone (figure 1).

3 Starting from the bicone, build the other half of the base as follows. String one 4-mm pearl, one 3-mm pearl, one 11°, one 3-mm pearl, and one 4-mm pearl and pass again through the bicone from which the thread exited. Pass through the next bicone. Add the next unit (one 4-mm pearl, one 3-mm pearl, one 11°) and weave

through the 3-mm and 4-mm pearl beads of the previous unit, then forward through the bicone from which the thread exited, and the next bicone too. After completing six units, weave in a circle through the six size 11° seed beads on top. The base is now finished.

4 In this step, you'll add the attachment beads. Starting from a size 11° seed bead, pick up one 15° and pass through the next 11°; repeat to add a total of six size 15°s to the circle, then weave forward to exit a bicone. String one 15°, one 11°, and one 15°, and pass through the next bicone; repeat five more times, then weave forward to the other half of the base and add six 15°s to the ring of 11°s at the center (figure 2).

5 With the thread exiting a size 15° seed bead on the inner circle, string two 15°s, one 3-mm pearl, and four 15°s, and then pass through the corresponding 11° at the equator of the base. String four 15°s, one 3-mm pearl, and two 15°s, and pass again through the 15° seed bead from which the thread exited to form one netting unit. Weave forward to exit the first 3-mm pearl added in this step. To build

the next netting unit, add four 15°s, pass through the next size 11° seed bead at the equator, string four 15°s, one 3-mm pearl, and two 15°s, weave through the next 15° at the inner ring, add two 15°s, and weave through the 3-mm pearl that was the starting point for this unit. Weave forward to the 3-mm pearl just added; this is where you'll start the next unit. The thread path will alternate between clockwise and counterclockwise from circle to circle (figure 3). After finishing the netting on this side, weave through the beadwork and repeat the same on the other half of the base. Be sure to bead this netting very tightly to give the piece stability.

Repeat steps 1 through 5 to make a second beaded bead. To assemble each into an earring, string one 4-mm pearl, a beaded bead, and one 4-mm pearl on an eye pin, and make a loop at the end. Attach three bell-shaped pendants to one end and an ear hook to the other end.

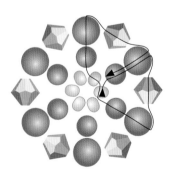

figure 1

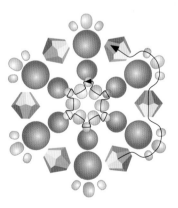

figure 2

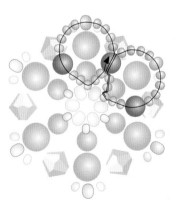

figure 3

96

NATHALIE PENDANT

This pendant is dedicated to my editor, Nathalie, who asked me one day if I could
make a square shape using the Scheherezade technique. Working on the types of
changes she requested was a real pleasure. (By the way, being mentioned by name
like this makes her blush to no end!)

1 Start by beading a strip of RAW units as follows. Begin with a unit of four 3-mm fire-polished beads. String three 4-mm fire-polished beads for the next unit. Add one 4-mm, one 3-mm, and one 4-mm fire-polished bead for the third unit (figure 1). Beginning with the bead outlined in green in figure 1, repeat the three units three more times, joining the last unit to the first to create a ring. The ring has four units of 3-mm fire-polished beads; the other units are made with 4-mm and 3-mm beads. The small units will form the inner sides of the square, and the vertical 4-mm beads form the inner corners of the square.

2 Starting from the top horizontal beads of the additional inner square (outlined in red in figure 2), build RAW units around the inner square as follows. Begin with the thread exiting a 3-mm fire-polished bead and add one RAW unit using 3-mm fire-polished beads. Going counterclockwise, add two 4-mm fire-polished beads for the next unit. Next, for the corner unit, add three 4-mm beads. Continue as shown in figure 2, then turn the beadwork over and repeat on the other side of the inner square.

3 In this step you'll zip the upper and lower flat squares together with RAW. Beginning at a corner, add one 8-mm round, then one 6-mm round, then one 4-mm fire-polished bead twice, then one 6-mm, and then one 8-mm round bead. Repeat in this manner until all sides are closed (figure 3).

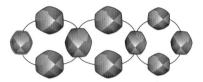

figure 1

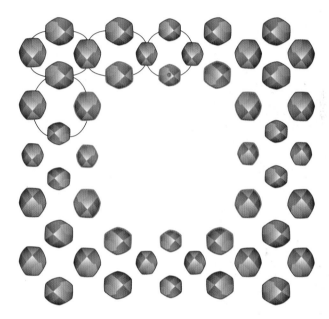

figure 2

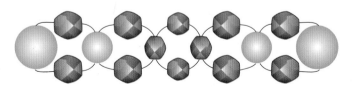

figure 3

4 Now you'll add beads in the gaps between the RAW units as follows. Beginning with the upper beads of the inner square, add one 8° in each corner and one 11° on each side of the 3-mm fire-polished beads. For the upper beads on the outer square, add one 11° on each side of the 3-mm fire-polished beads, one 8° in the next gap between two 4-mm fire-polished beads, then in the corners add a picot of one 11°, one 8°, and one 11°; then weave along the next side. When the outer square is finished, turn the beadwork over and repeat the same steps on the other side (figure 4).

5 Now you'll add netting between the beads added in step 4. Refer to figure 5 when working steps 5 and 6. Starting from the first 11° at the inner square, *string two 15°s, one 11°, and two 15°s, and pass through the next 11° in the inner square, creating an arc. For the next arc, string two 15°s, one 11°, and three 15°s, and pass through the 8° seed bead at the corner of the inner square. Make an arc of three 15°s, one 11°, and two 15°s, and pass through the next 11°. The beads added in this row are outlined in red in figure 5. Repeat from * until the square is completed. Weave forward so the thread exits the 11° seed bead in the middle of the first arc.

6 In the next row, the arcs are attached to the outer square. String two 15°s and pass through the corresponding 11° on the outer square. String two 15°s and pass through the 11° of the next arc. String two 15°s and pass through the 8° seed bead in front of the corner. String one 11°, one 4-mm bicone, and one 11°, skip the corner beads, and pass through the next size 8° seed bead. Continue in this fashion until the square is completed. The beads in this step are outlined in green. Repeat the same netting on the other side of the beadwork.

7 Refer to figure 6 as you work this step and be sure to maintain good tension throughout. The netting on the outside edge is attached in a circular fashion, forming rings. Begin with the thread exiting the 11° to the left of the 3-mm fire-polished bead in the middle, shown at the top of figure 6 with a red dot. For the first ring, bead counterclockwise as follows. String two 15°s, one 8°, and two 15°s, and weave through the 11°, the fire-polished bead, and the 11° on the bottom. Again string two 15°s, one 8°, and two 15°s, and weave through the 11°, the fire-polished bead, and the 11° on top. Weave forward so the thread exits the next 8° in this circle.

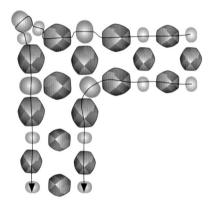

figure 4

figure 5

Bead clockwise for the next ring. String three 15°s and pass through the 8° on the bottom. String two 15°s, one 3-mm bicone, one 8°, one 3-mm bicone, and two 15°s; pass through the 8° on the top. String three 15°s and pass through the 8° seed bead that served as the starting point of this ring. If you had difficulty maintaining the thread tension, weave again through all the beads in the rings. Weave forward so the thread exits the 8° between the two bicones just added.

String one 3-mm bicone, one 11°, and one 15°; pass through the 8° seed bead in the corner picot. String one 15°, one 11°, one 3-mm bicone, one 8°, one 3-mm bicone, one 11°, and one 15°, then pass through the 8° in the corner picot (bottom); complete the ring with one 15°, one 11°, and one 3-mm bicone.

Weave forward so the thread exits the last 8° added in the previous row. To add the loop after the corner, work clockwise to add one 3-mm bicone, two 15°s, one 8°, three 15°s, one 8°, three 15°s, one 8°, two 15°s, and one 3-mm bicone; pass through the 8° where this ring started.

Continue adding netting until the whole outside edge is covered. If there are gaps between the beads, weave through again and fill them with 15°s.

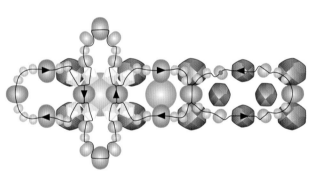

figure 6

SUPPLIES

192 blue-green fire-polished
beads, 4 mm

210 blue-green fire-polished
beads, 3 mm

18 light green glass pearls, 6 mm

Size 11° silver seed beads, 2 g

72 size 8° silver seed beads

24 silver fire-polished beads, 3 mm

Size 15° metallic green
seed beads, 5 g

FireLine, smoke, 6-pound test

Size 12 beading needle

Small sharp scissors

FINISHED SIZE

Interior circumference,
7½ inches (19 cm)

SCHEHEREZADE BANGLE

I designed this bangle using the techniques I developed for the Scheherezade
Pendant (page 91). A little advice: Bead that pendant first to get familiar with the
technique. A simple change in bead sizes produces a fancy hexagonal bangle.
The number of rows is the same as for the pendant.

1 Using 3-mm and 4-mm blue-green fire-polished beads, bead a row of 42 RAW units following the sequence shown in figure 1 six times. Attach the last unit to the first unit through the bead outlined on the left of the figure. (**Note:** The outlined bead is a side bead in both the first and the last RAW units.) This ring is the inner circle of the bangle.

2 On one side of the ring, use 3- and 4-mm blue-green fire-polished beads and glass pearls to add two RAW rows as shown in the upper part of figure 2. (The beads of the starting circle are outlined in red. As described in step 1, the beads outlined in black belong to the first and last units.) Weave back to the base ring and work one row of RAW on the other side of the ring as shown in the lower part of figure 2. The next row is the zipping row; only the vertical beads are added (outlined in green) to close the tube and form a bangle. Add a vertical bead and pass through the corresponding horizontal bead on the opposite side until all beads in the outer rows are joined. The row with the round beads is now the equator on the outside of the bangle.

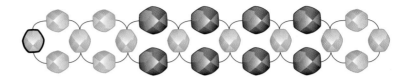

figure 1

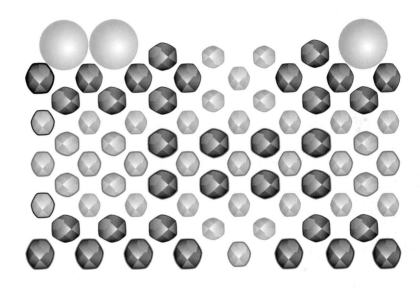

figure 2

▶ Stitch in the Ditch

Starting on the inner ring, add size 11° beads between the horizontal 3-mm fire-polished beads and size 8° beads between the horizontal 4-mm fire-polished beads, as shown on the bottom row of figure 3. In the next row of horizontal beads, add size 8° beads between all the fire-polished beads, as shown in the middle row of figure 3. In the last row, add 3-mm silver fire-polished beads on both sides of all the glass pearls, size 8° beads between the 3- and 4-mm blue-green fire-polished beads, and size 11° beads between two 3-mm fire-polished beads as shown in the top row of figure 3. Repeat the first and the second rows on the other side of the beadwork.

▶ Netting

There are two kinds of netting rows. First you'll create a row of arcs between the ditch beads of one row added in the previous step, and then you'll attach those arcs to the ditch beads in the next row. Refer to figure 4 for all netting steps; the arcs are outlined in red, while the beads of the attaching rows are outlined in green.

1 For the first row of arcs, begin with the thread exiting a ditch bead in the inner ring. String two 15°s, one 11°, and two 15°s, and pass through the next ditch bead. The beads for this row are shown with a red outline at the bottom of figure 4. Repeat until the ring is complete; at the end weave through the beadwork so the thread exits from the size 11° seed bead in the first arc added.

2 String two 15°s and pass through the size 8° ditch bead to the right in the next row; string two 15°s and pass through the 11° in the next arc. The added beads are in the second row from the bottom in figure 4, shown with a green outline. Continue in this fashion until the ring is complete. Weave through the beadwork to exit the size 8° bead in the first connection. For the next row, add three 15°s, one 11°, and three 15°s for the arcs directly below the RAW units containing pearls, and add two 15°s, one 11°, and two 15°s for the other arcs. The beads added in this row are shown third from the bottom, outlined in red, in figure 4.

3 The last connecting row requires varying numbers of 15° beads. Add four 15°s to connect an arc to the silver fire-polished beads on each side of the pearls; add three 15°s to connect an arc to the silver fire-polished beads between the glass pearls and the 4-mm fire-polished beads, and add two 15°s to connect an arc to a size 8° or 11° ditch bead. Continue in this fashion until the ring is finished, then repeat the steps on the other side of the bangle.

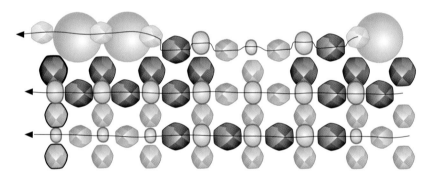

figure 3

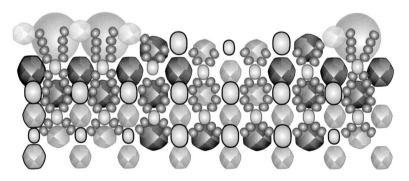

figure 4

CHAPTER 5
PEARL CENTERS

Pearls or round beads are the focal points of the beadwork shown in this chapter.

Whether you use them as the foundation for a design, connect them

with netting, or simply bezel them, pearls are indispensable.

SPIKEY TOPS BRACELET

This bracelet combines large round beads and sparkling crystals in a beautiful construction. With its dimensional shape, it will get noticed for sure. You can create an interesting contrast by playing matte round beads off the shimmer of the crystals.

1 String one 6-mm round bead and one fire-polished bead; repeat three more times for a total of eight beads, then pass through the first bead strung to create a ring. Weave twice through the ring to secure the thread. End with the thread exiting a fire-polished bead.

2 String three 15°s, one 11°, and three 15° seed beads; skip the round bead and weave through the next fire-polished bead, forming an arc above the round bead. Repeat three more times to work completely around the ring. End with the thread exiting a size 11° seed bead (figure 1).

3 Pick up one 4-mm pearl and weave through the 11° seed bead in the next arc. Repeat three more times to complete the ring. The arcs pull to the middle in this

step. Weave again through the beads in this row to secure the thread. End with the thread exiting an 11° seed bead (figure 2).

4 String two 15°s, one 11°, and two 15°s, skip the pearl, and pass through the next 11°, forming an arc above the pearl. Repeat three more times to work completely around the ring. Weave forward so the thread exits an 11° added in this row (figure 3).

5 Pick up one 3-mm bicone and pass through the 11° in the next arc. Repeat three more times to work completely around the ring. Weave twice through the beads in this row, then weave back to the beads in the first row so the thread exits a 6-mm round bead (figure 4).

SUPPLIES

34 gold satin round beads, 6 mm

44 dark bronze fire-polished beads, 4 mm

44 powder green glass pearls, 4 mm

Size 15° light gold seed beads, 3 g

Size 11° dark berry seed beads, 2 g

44 jet black 2XAB crystal bicones, 3 mm

20 jet black 2XAB crystal bicones, 4 mm

2 copper jump rings, 5–7 mm

1 copper magnetic clasp

FireLine, 6-pound test

Size 12 beading needle

Small sharp scissors

2 pairs of flat-nose pliers

FINISHED SIZE

7¾ inches (19.7 cm), not including clasp

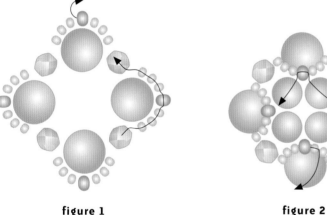

figure 1

figure 2

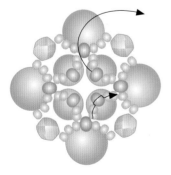

figure 3

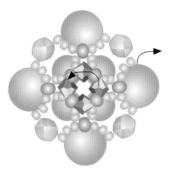

figure 4

6 Refer to figure 5 as you work steps 6 and 7. Build another component like the one described in steps 1 through 5, but use the 6-mm round bead from which the thread exited in step 5 as one of the beads of the basic ring for this component. After finishing the second unit, weave forward through the connecting 6-mm round bead. String one 11°, one 4-mm bicone, and three 15°s; weave back through the bicone, the 11°, and the 6-mm round to form a fringe. Build the same fringe on the other side of the connecting bead (figure 5). Continue in this fashion until your bracelet reaches the desired length. The sample shown has 11 components.

7 At the beginning and the end, make an arc above the 6-mm round bead with four 15°s, one 11°, and four 15°s. With the thread exiting the 11° in this arc, make a loop of five 11°s. Pass through the loop again, filling the four gaps between the beads in the loop with 15°s. Weave several times through the beads in the arc and the loop to secure and strengthen them. Attach the clasp to the loops with jump rings.

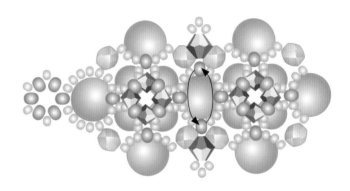

figure 5

Alternate Colorway

VOLCANOES NECKLACE

Each bezeled element of this necklace reminds me of a little Krakatoa or Vesuvius. Bezeled beads or stones can be connected in so many different ways—not only in a curve, but also straight, as several straight parallel lines, or in dimensional bodies such as cubes or spheres. Depending on your color choices, these volcanoes can look either casual or fancy.

108

SUPPLIES

22 greenish brown round
African opal beads, 6 mm

Size 11° bronze cylinder beads, 10 g

Size 11° bronze seed beads, 5 g

Size 15° light bronze seed beads, 5 g

1 antique bronze lobster clasp

2 bronze jump rings, 5 mm

FireLine, 6-pound test

Small sharp scissors

2 pairs of flat-nose pliers

FINISHED SIZE

15¾ inches (40 cm) long,
not including clasp

1 String one 6-mm round, five cylinder beads, one 11° seed bead, and five cylinder beads; pass again through the round bead and position the other beads so they form an arc around one side of the round bead. Weave again through the ring to secure the thread. String five more cylinder beads, one 11°, and five cylinder beads. Pass again through the 6-mm round bead and position this set of beads so they form an arc on the other side of the round bead. Weave forward through the beads of the second arc so the thread exits a cylinder bead in front of the round bead. Pick up one 11° and weave through the other arc, exiting in front of the round bead. Add one 11° and weave forward through the next five cylinder beads (figure 1).

2 Pick up one 11° seed bead, skip the 11° seed bead from the previous row, and weave through the next five cylinder beads. Repeat three more times until you've worked completely around the ring. Weave forward so the thread exits the first 11° added in this step (figure 2).

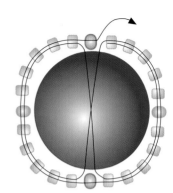

figure 1

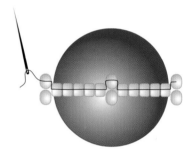

figure 2

3 String five 15°s, skip the cylinder beads, and pass through the next 11° added in step 2. Repeat three more times, then weave once more through the beads in this row to secure the thread and achieve good tension; there should be no gaps between the beads in the ring. Weave forward to the 11°s added in step 1 and add five 15°s between each. At the end weave forward so the thread exits a cylinder bead in front of the gap between the two size 11° seed beads (figure 3).

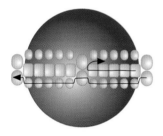

figure 3

4 Refer to figure 4 for steps 4 through 7. In this step, you'll create the picot row. String one 15°, one 11°, and one 15°; weave through the next five cylinder beads. Repeat three more times as you work completely around the ring. At the end, weave forward so the thread exits the 11° in the first picot (the beads in this row are outlined in red in figure 4).

5 String seven cylinder beads (outlined in green in figure 4), then pass through the 11° in the next picot. Repeat three more times. If you tend to have loose thread tension, weave again through this row to secure the thread. Weave forward to exit a cylinder bead in front of a size 11° seed bead.

6 Add a picot of one 15°, one 11°, and one 15°, as outlined in blue in figure 4, and weave through the next seven cylinder beads. Repeat three more times as you bead around the ring. At the end, weave forward so the thread exits an 11° seed bead in a picot added in this step.

7 String four cylinder beads and pass through the fourth of the seven cylinder beads added in step 5. String four cylinder beads and weave through the 11° in the next picot. Repeat three more times as you bead completely around the ring.

8 The purpose of this final row is to embellish the edges. With the thread exiting a cylinder bead in front of an 11° in a picot added in step 6, add another picot as before (one 15°, one 11°, and one 15°), weave through the next four cylinder beads, add an 11°, and weave through the next four cylinder beads. Repeat three more times to complete the ring (figure 5). Secure the thread and cut it off.

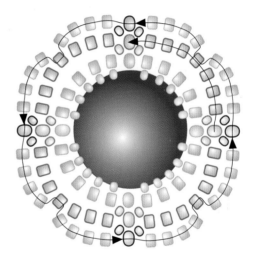

figure 4

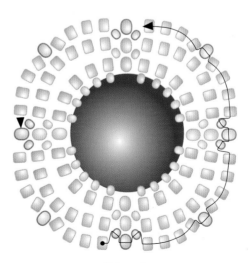

figure 5

Repeat steps 1 through 8 to make 21 more components, connecting each one as it's finished, as follows.

9 Refer to figure 6 for the remaining steps. To attach the components in the curved shape of the necklace, build one connection between two adjacent 11° seed beads in the picots at the corners, and a second connection between two adjacent 11° seed beads on the side of the units.

With the thread exiting an 11° in one picot, pass through the 11° in the adjacent picot, string two 11°s, and pass again through the bead from which the thread originally exited. Weave a second time through all four beads, then add one size 15° seed bead in each of the four gaps between the 11°s. Weave a second time through the beads added in this step to strengthen the connection.

10 Weave forward to exit the 11° seed bead on the side of the unit. String one 15°, one cylinder bead, one 15°, and (at the "open" side of the connection) pass through the 11° seed bead in the adjacent

unit. Pick up one cylinder bead and pass again through the 11° seed bead from which the thread originally exited. Weave twice more through the six beads in this connection, then secure the thread and cut it off.

11 At both ends of the beading, add a loop of six 11° seed beads onto the picot in the inner corner. Weave through the loop again, adding one 15° in each of the five gaps between the 11°s. Use a jump ring to hang the lobster clasp to one loop, and attach a jump ring to the other loop.

▶ **Variation**

If you want to create a straight bracelet, make at least seven components. Measure the fit, factoring in the clasp, and make more as desired. Then, instead of attaching them as described in steps 9 and 10, simply join them at both corners or at the sides. Note that the latter is a more delicate connection.

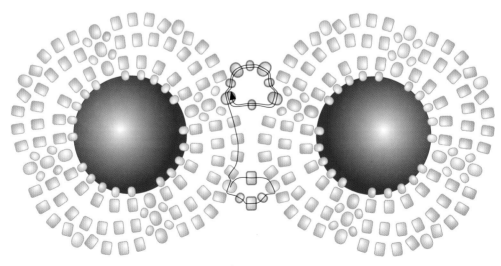

figure 6

PURPLE ROPE NECKLACE

This rope is kind of an endless Scheherezade. While experimenting with the Scheherezade Bangle, I kept wondering how I might connect the beads to make the finished piece flexible. Purple Rope Necklace is made of two different beaded beads, a long one and a short one, that are covered and joined together with netting. If you want to make a bangle, I recommend you use only the small beaded beads.

SUPPLIES

235 silver fire-polished beads, 3 mm

250 iris purple fire-polished beads, 4 mm

85 lavender glass pearls, 6 mm

Size 11° silver seed beads, 8 g

Size 15° silver seed beads, 15 g

Size 8° iris purple seed beads, 4 g

2 silver jump rings, 4 mm

1 silver clasp

FireLine, 6-pound test

Size 12 beading needle

Small sharp scissors

2 pairs of flat-nose pliers

FINISHED SIZE

17½ inches (44.5 cm), not including clasp

▶ Small Beaded Bead

1 String five 3-mm fire-polished beads and pass through the first bead strung to form a ring. Weave twice more through all the beads. This forms the base ring.

2 String one 4-mm fire-polished bead, one pearl, and one 4-mm fire-polished bead. Weave again through the bead from which the thread originally exited, then forward through the next bead in the basic ring (figure 1). *String one 4-mm fire-polished bead and one pearl, then weave through the fire-polished bead from the previous step and the one in the base ring from which the thread originally exited, then weave forward through the next bead in the basic ring. Repeat from * until you've made four RAW units. The last unit will close the circle. After the fourth unit, weave forward through the 4-mm fire-polished bead in the first unit. Pick up one pearl and weave again through all four beads in the last unit. End with the thread exiting a pearl. Weave twice through the five pearls; they serve as the base ring for the next row of five RAW units.

3 String one 4-mm, one 3-mm, and one 4-mm fire-polished bead and pass again through the pearl from which the thread exited. Weave forward through the next pearl. Continue making RAW units until the row is finished. At the end, weave once through the five 3-mm fire-polished beads. The base of the small bead is now finished.

4 In the second layer, you'll fill the gaps at the crossing points of the base. The first group will be added in a horizontal circle. With the thread exiting a 3-mm fire-polished bead, pick up one 11° and pass through the next 3-mm fire-polished bead. Repeat four more times to complete the ring. Pass through a 4-mm fire-polished bead, pick up one 3-mm fire-polished bead, and weave down through the next 4-mm fire-polished bead (vertically). Weave forward through a 3-mm fire-polished bead, then up through the next 4-mm bead. Add one 3-mm bead, and then weave up through the next 4-mm bead. Continue like this until you've covered the five crossing points in the middle of the bead. At the other end of the bead, add one 11° seed bead between each of the five 3-mm fire-polished beads. Figure 2 shows a partial view of the side of the bead.

5 The next layer is netting that's connected only to the beads in the second layer, which were added in step 4. For the small beads there are three netting rows. With the thread exiting an 11°, string two 15°s, one 11°, and two 15°s, and pass through the next 11° to form an arc. Repeat to build four more arcs, then weave forward so the thread exits the 11° in the first arc (the beads are outlined in red in figure 3, which is a side view).

Now you'll bead rings around the pearls (outlined in green in figure 3). String three 15°s and one 11°, then pass through the next 3-mm fire-polished bead. *String one 11°, three 15°s, one 11°, three 15°s, and one 11°, and pass through the 3-mm fire-polished bead on the other side of the pearl, forming a large arc around the pearl. Complete the ring by adding one 11° and three 15°s, and pass through the 11° where

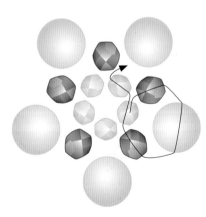

figure 1

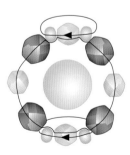

figure 2

the ring started. Weave forward to a 3-mm fire-polished bead beside the next pearl, which is the starting point for the ring. **Note:** The rings around this and the next three pearls begin from a fire-polished bead instead of an arc—it's just easier this way. Bead rings around the four pearls, then weave forward so the thread exits an 11° of the large arc around the pearl. String two 15°s and pass through the 11° in the ring at the end. String two 15°s and weave through the 11° in the next large arc (these beads are outlined in purple in figure 3). Repeat four more times to complete the ring. The small bead is now finished.

▶ Large Beaded Bead

1 These are beaded in basically the same way as the small beads, but the number of RAW rows is larger. Begin with five 3-mm fire-polished beads in the basic ring, as you did for the small bead. For the first unit in the first row, string one 3-mm, one 4-mm, and one 3-mm fire-polished bead. Continue the row as described in step 2 on page 112. At the end, weave through the five 4-mm fire-polished beads on top.

For the first unit in the second row, string one 4-mm fire-polished bead, one pearl, and one 4-mm fire-polished bead. Continue as for the previous the row and at the end weave through the five pearls. Now bead a third row with only 4-mm fire-polished beads, and a fourth row with only 3-mm fire-polished beads.

For the next layer, add one 11° (horizontal) between each of the five 3-mm fire-polished beads. In the next horizontal line, add one 8° between each of the five 4-mm fire-polished beads. In the middle of the bead, add 3-mm fire-polished beads in a vertical direction, as shown in figure 4. Add one 8° between each of the 4-mm fire-polished beads in the next horizontal layer, then one 11° between each of the 3-mm fire-polished beads in the last horizontal layer.

2 Refer to figure 5 to add netting to the bead as follows. With the thread exiting a 3-mm fire-polished bead, string two 15°s,

one 11°, and two 15°s; pass through the 3-mm fire-polished bead again to form an arc. Repeat four more times around the bead. Weave forward so the thread exits the 11° in the first arc. The beads added in this step are those at the top of the illustration, outlined in red.

For the second row, string two 15°s, pass through the 8°, string two 15°s, and weave through the 11° in the next arc. Repeat until the ring is finished and end with the thread exiting an 8° seed bead. The beads added in this step are near the top of the illustration, outlined in green.

The third row is another row of arcs. String three 15°s, one 11°, and three 15°s, and pass through the next 8°, forming an arc. Repeat four more times to finish the ring; end with the thread exiting the 11° in the first arc added in this row. The beads added in this step are above the center of the illustration, outlined in red.

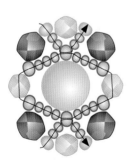

figure 3

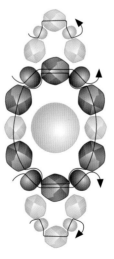

figure 4

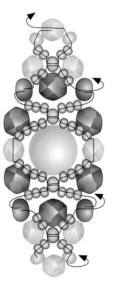

figure 5

The next row adds arcs around the pearls. Starting from the 11°, string four 15°s and pass down through the vertical 3-mm fire-polished bead. String four 15°s, one 11°, and four 15°s, and pass through the 3-mm fire-polished bead on the other side of the pearl. Complete the ring by stringing four 15°s, then pass through the 11° where the ring started. The beads added in this step are around the center pearl, outlined in green. Weave forward through the 3-mm fire-polished bead. **Note:** The rings around this and the next three pearls begin from a fire-polished bead instead of an arc—it's just easier this way. Bead rings around the four pearls, then weave forward so the thread exits an 11° in the large arc around the pearl.

String three 15°s and pass through the 8° in the next horizontal ring, then string three 15°s and pass through the 11° in the large arc around the next pearl. Repeat four more times to complete the ring. The beads added in this step are just below the center, outlined in red. End with the thread exiting an 8° bead in the ring.

The next row is another arc row. String two 15°s, one 11°, and two 15°s, and pass through the next 8°, forming an arc. Repeat four more times around the ring. The beads added in this step are near the bottom, outlined in green. Weave forward to exit an 11° bead in an arc.

In the last row, connect the arcs to the 11°s on the base as follows. String two 15°s and pass through the next 11° on the base ring, then string two 15°s and pass through the 11° in the next arc. The beads added in this step are at the bottom of the illustration, outlined in red. Repeat four more times to complete the ring.

▶ **Join the Beads**

1 Attach the large bead to the small one with simple netting as follows. Starting from the size 11° seed beads of the large bead (the ones in the base ring, between the 3-mm fire-polished beads), string two 15°s, one 11°, and two 15°s; pass through the next 11°, forming an arc. Repeat four more times. Weave forward so the thread exits the 11° in the first arc. Add a second and third row of arcs (with the same bead count) attached to the 11°s in the previous arc.

With the fourth row, attach the netting to the short bead as follows. With the thread exiting an 11° in an arc in the last row added, string two 15°s and pass through the 11° on the base ring of the small beaded bead. String two 15°s and pass through the 11° in the next arc. Repeat until the netting is attached to the previous bead.

2 Continue beading, alternating small and large beads, attaching each to the previous one. The necklace shown consists of nine small and eight large beads.

3 To attach the clasp, you'll need to add two short arcs of beads to each of the open ends of the first and last sections. Each strand is made of six 15° seed beads woven between the 11°s of the second layer. Attach the jump rings to the strands, then attach the clasp ends to the jump rings.

SABINE LIPPERT'S BEADED FANTASIES

SUPPLIES

Size 11° light golden seed beads, 1.5 g

11 golden size 8° seed beads

22 mauve satin round beads, 6 mm

Size 15° seed beads:

Light golden, 1.5 g

Violet, 1 g

11 red AB satin crystal bicones, 4 mm

11 bronze drop beads, 3.4 mm

1 amethyst rivoli, 14 mm

1 pin back

FireLine, 6-pound test

Size 12 beading needle

Small sharp scissors

FINISHED SIZE

2 inches (5.1 cm) in diameter

GRANADA BROOCH

One of my most popular patterns, Granada takes a step away from the usual method of bezeling a stone. I don't start with one ring of beads that I later embellish—quite the opposite. The first step is a halo of embellishment to which the stone is later attached.

The disk is made up of 11 sequences based on RAW.

1 String one size 11° seed bead, one size 8° seed bead, one 11°, one 6-mm round, one 11°, one 6-mm round, one 11°, and one 6-mm round; pass through the first bead strung to create a ring. Weave through the beads again to secure the thread, exiting the first 11° strung (figure 1).

2 String three violet 15°s, skip the 8° bead, and pass through the next 11°. String two violet 15°s, one 11°, one bicone, one 11°, and two violet 15°s; skip the round bead and weave through the next 11°, creating an arc around the round bead on the left. For the next arc, string five violet 15°s, one 11°, and five more violet 15°s. Skip the round bead and pass though the next 11°. String two violet 15°s and one 11°, and pass back through the bicone. String one 11° and two 15°s, again skip the round bead, and pass through the next 11°. Weave forward to exit the next 15° (figure 2).

3 Pick up one golden 15° and pass through the next violet 15°. Repeat this step, then weave forward through the next 11° and the round bead, then through the two 15°s and one 11° seed bead (heading to the middle); the thread exits in front of the bicone. Pick up one drop bead, and weave forward to the other side through the next 11°, the two 15°s, and along the next arc through the five 15°s; the thread exits in front of the size 11° seed bead. String five golden 15°s, skip the 11°, and weave forward through the next five 15°s (the five golden beads form a peak). Weave through the next 11° and the next round bead (figure 3).

4 Starting from this round bead, build 10 more units the same way, with the basic ring first, then the embellishment. As you make the eleventh unit, close the ring by using the round in the first unit for the basic ring in this unit. Weave forward to the middle of the ring so the thread exits the first golden 15° of the small arc above the 8°. String three golden 15°s and pass through the next golden 15°.

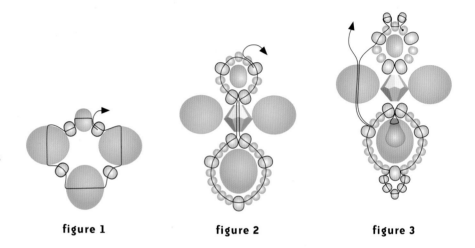

figure 1   figure 2   figure 3

Weave forward through the first golden 15° in the next unit. Repeat this step 10 more times until the ring is finished. To strengthen the inner circle, weave again through the beads in this row—*not* through the beads in the previous steps but only through the groups of three beads added in this step. The beads will form little peaks, heading to the middle (figure 4). It's important to have good tension in this step—if the beads are connected too loosely, they won't hold the rivoli in place.

5 Weave to the back of the beadwork and exit a size 8° bead. String three 11°s and pass through the next 8°. Pull the 8°s a bit to the back—this imparts a dimensional appearance to the piece. Repeat this 10 more times. Weave forward so the thread exits the second of the next three 11°s. String two violet 15°s and pass through the second 11° in the next group of three. Repeat this 10 more times. Place the rivoli face down into the cup you've just created, then weave again through the beads in this row. You'll have to pull the thread hard to close this ring; the beads should be tightly side by side. (If your thread tension was too loose, the rivoli won't be properly secured. In this case, use a 16-mm rivoli instead.) With the thread exiting a group of two 15°s, pick up a golden 15° and weave through the next two violet 15°s. Repeat this step 10 more times (figure 5).

6 Attach the pin back with a new thread. Should the component get twisted or damaged later, you can then cut it off easily and replace it without damaging the rest of the beadwork.

Reverse side

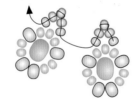

figure 4

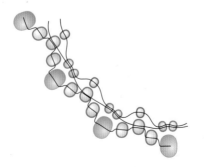

figure 5

SUPPLIES

16 champagne glass pearls, 3 mm

16 champagne glass pearls, 4 mm

20 turquoise 2XAB crystal bicones, 3 mm

2 turquoise 2XAB crystal chatons, 8 mm

Size 15° seed beads:

　Light gold, 2 g

　Metallic dark raspberry, 2 g

Size 11° dark bronze seed beads, 1 g

2 golden ear wires

FireLine, 6-pound test

Small sharp scissors

2 pairs of flat-nose pliers

FINISHED SIZE

2 inches (5.1 cm),
not including ear wires

GRANADA EARRINGS

I was asked to make some earrings based on my Granada brooch. Simply using smaller beads wasn't possible. It became quite the challenge! But challenges drive me, and I'm not one to give up easily.

1 Build a ring of eight RAW units as follows. For the first unit, string one 3-mm pearl, one bicone, one 3-mm pearl, one raspberry 15°, one 4-mm pearl, and one raspberry 15°. Pass through the first bead added to form a ring, then weave through all the beads again, ending with the thread exiting the first 3-mm pearl added. String one bicone, one 3-mm pearl, one raspberry 15°, one 4-mm pearl, and one raspberry 15°; pass again through the 3-mm pearl from which the thread exited. Weave forward to the 3-mm pearl added in this unit and repeat until you have eight units; the eighth unit shares a bead with the first unit to form a ring. Weave a second time through the beads in the last unit to secure the thread (figure 1).

2 Weave through the ring of bicones and add one 11° seed bead in each ditch between the bicones. Weave a second time through the beads in this ring to secure the thread.

3 To create the beaded cross-stitches, begin with the thread exiting a 3-mm pearl from inside the ring toward the outside. Pass through the size 15°, then string three gold, one raspberry, and two gold 15°s; cross over the unit and pass through the other 3-mm pearl in this unit, working from the inside to the outside. Pass through the next 15°, string three gold 15°s, pass through the raspberry 15° in the first half of the cross, string two gold 15°s, and pass again through the first 3-mm pearl, working from the inside to the outside, and finally pass through the next 15°. String six gold 15°s, skip the 4-mm pearl, and pass through the 15° on the other side of that pearl. The six beads form an arc

around the 4-mm pearl (figure 2). Weave forward through the 3-mm pearl, the bicone, one 11°, the next bicone, and the next 3-mm pearl, working from the inside to the outside. Begin the next crossing and repeat until all units are covered in cross-stitch. At the end, weave forward so the thread exits the third of six size 15°s, forming the arc around a 4-mm pearl.

4 Refer to figure 3 on the next page as you do this step. Turn the beadwork over. Pick up one raspberry 15°, weave through the next three gold and one raspberry 15°s, then through the 3-mm pearl, working

from the outside to the inside. String five raspberry 15°s, and weave back through the first and second of them and then through the 3-mm pearl—the seed beads form a little fringe on the back. Weave forward to exit the third bead in the next arc of six beads. Repeat until eight fringes are complete. Weave forward to exit the top bead in one fringe, pick up one gold 15°, and pass through the top bead in the next fringe. Repeat seven more times until the ring is complete. Loosen the thread and place the chaton into the ring upside-down. Pull the thread up taut and

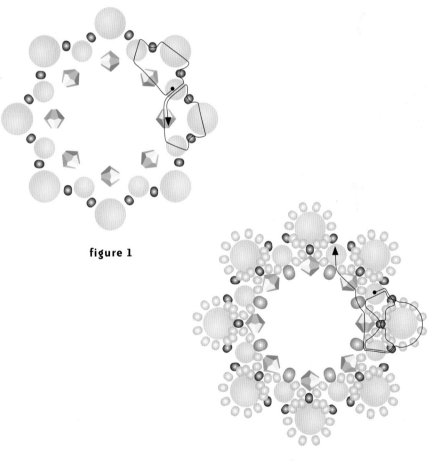

figure 1

figure 2

weave several times through the beads in this ring. Weave through the beadwork so the thread exits the raspberry 15° in the middle of an arc around a 4-mm pearl.

5 From this bead you'll bead a strip of RAW to which you'll mount the ear wire. Start the strip with four RAW units made with raspberry 15°s. For the next unit,

string one raspberry 15°, one bicone, and three raspberry 15°s; pass back through the bicone, pick up one more raspberry 15°, and pass through the 15° at the top of the four-unit strip (figure 4). Weave forward to the 15° at the top of the unit with the bicone, and weave four more units of RAW using raspberry 15°s. At the end of the strip, build a loop with seven gold 15°s. Weave along the outside of the strip and add one gold 15° in each ditch between the raspberry 15°s. At the bicone, add a group of four raspberry 15°s. Weave along the outside of the strip below the bicone, adding one gold 15° in each ditch between the raspberry 15°s. Work up the other side, adding four raspberry 15°s on the other side of the bicone, and continue along the other strip. When you reach the loop, add gold 15°s in the gaps between the loop beads. Weave back along the outside to the middle of the group of four beads on one side of the bicone. Add one gold 15°, weave forward to the other side

of the bicone, and add another gold 15° (figure 5). Pass through the bicone (heading in the direction of the pendant) and string three gold 15°s, one bicone, and three gold 15°s. Weave back through the bicone, the three 15° beads, and the next bicone (thus making a fringe). Secure the thread and cut it off.

6 Attach an ear wire through the loop at the top of the strip.

Repeat all steps to make a second earring.

This shows the strip of RAW to which the ear wire is attached from the loop at the top.

figure 3

figure 4

figure 5

SPARKLING TOPS NECKLACE

Depending on the way you connect these sparkling elements, you can create

a long curve for a perfectly fitting necklace or a straight line of units for a bracelet.

SUPPLIES

Size 11° galvanized gold seed beads, 8 g

78 metallic blue round beads, 6 mm

116 flax gold fire-polished beads, 3 mm

Size 15° galvanized gold seed beads, 8 g

96 jet black 2XAB crystal bicones, 3 mm

152 jet black 2XAB crystal bicones, 4 mm

76 size 8° metallic green seed beads

2 golden jump rings, 5 mm

1 golden clasp

FireLine, smoke, 6-pound test

Size 12 beading needle

Small sharp scissors

2 pairs of flat-nose pliers

FINISHED SIZE

18½ inches (47 cm), not including clasp

The necklace is built in a continuous series of links and units, with links at the beginning and at the end for attaching the clasp.

1 String one size 11° seed bead, one round bead, two 11°s, one fire-polished bead, two 11°s, one round, one 11°, and one fire-polished bead, and pass through the first bead strung to form a ring. Weave through the beads in the ring again, exiting an 11° just before a fire-polished bead. String four 15°s, skip the fire-polished bead, and weave through the beadwork until you reach the next fire-polished bead. Add four 15°s, skip the fire-polished bead, and weave through the beadwork to exit just before a round bead. As you can see in figure 1, there's a smaller group of beads between the round beads on top. This short side will be at the inner circle of the necklace, and the lower and larger group of five beads will be at the outer circle. The thread should exit before the round that follows the smaller bead group.

2 String two 15°s, one 11°, one 3-mm bicone, one 11°, and two 15°s; skip the round bead and weave through the next two 11°s and the next two 15°s. Pick up one 11° and weave through the next four beads (two 15°s and two 11°s). String two 15°s and one 11° and pass through the bicone. String one 11° and two 15°s, and pass through the 11° bead after the round bead (figure 2). You've finished making the first link.

3 Now you'll make the first unit. Weave through the beadwork so the thread exits a round bead. String [one 11°, one 8°, one 11°, one round] three times, then string one 11°, one 8°, and one 11°; pass through the round from which the thread exited to create a ring. Weave again through the beads in the ring, exiting an 11° before a

round bead. String one 4-mm bicone, one fire-polished bead, and one 4-mm bicone; skip the round bead and weave through the next three beads (an 11°, an 8°, and an 11°). Repeat three more times; weave forward so the thread exits a fire-polished bead (figure 3).

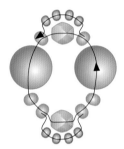

figure 1

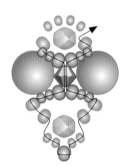

figure 2

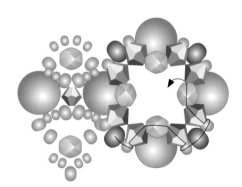

figure 3

4 Pick up one 3-mm bicone and pass through the next fire-polished bead. Repeat three more times and weave again through all the beads in this ring. With the thread exiting a fire-polished bead, pull the thread to secure the beads in the middle of the ring. String four 15°s, then pass through the next fire-polished bead. Repeat three more times. Weave forward so the thread exits the second of four size 15°s. Pick up one 11°, then weave forward to the middle of the next group of four size 15°s. Repeat three more times (figure 4).

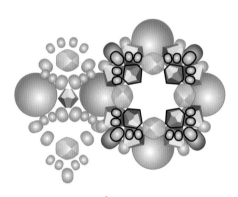

figure 4

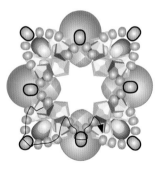

figure 5

5 The 4-mm bicones are in a vertical position now. In this step, you'll weave through these bicones up and down in a chainlike fashion. With the thread exiting a fire-polished bead, pass down through the next 4-mm bicone; string six 15°s and pass upward through the next 4-mm bicone, then through the next fire-polished bead. Pick up four 15°s, skip the fire-polished bead, and pass down through the next 4-mm bicone. Repeat these steps until you've passed through all the 4-mm bicones, creating four arcs with four size 15° seed beads on the top and four arcs with six size 15° seed beads at the base. Weave through the bicones and 15°s again and add one 11° bead in the middle of each arc (figure 5).

6 Weave forward to exit the round bead opposite the link, which is where you'll start the next link and after that the next unit. Be careful to bead the short parts of the links all on the same side. Continue until you have 20 links and 19 units made.

▶ Add the Clasp

Now you'll make loops on the beginning and ending links for mounting the clasp.

With the thread exiting the round bead, string three or four 15°s, one 11°, and another three or four 15°s, then pass through the round bead again. Weave twice through the beads added in this step, ending with the thread exiting from the 11° bead in the middle of the arc. Make a loop of five 11°s. Weave several times through the beads in the loop and fill the gaps between the beads with 15°s. You'll notice gaps on the left and right sides of the arc, and there's a little trick to covering them. Weave through the beads to the end of the arc. String as many beads as you need to fill the gap, then weave forward through the two 15°s, one 11°, one bicone, and the next three seed beads to the other side of the arc. Fill the gap, and weave again through the arc. Secure the thread and cut it off.

CHAPTER 6

SABINATION NATION,

OR HOW ONE BEADER APPROACHES DESIGN

It's not easy to describe the way I design my jewelry. I don't have a preferred colorway or a favorite technique. My projects are never planned; they're more like ideas in my head that I let grow. One project often leads to the next. Each technique contains the potential for further development, and I'll explain this through some examples. This chapter is meant to encourage you to allow your own projects to evolve through trial and error.

Three Crosses Necklace

Just yesterday, a friend who's an engineer asked me, "How do you manage to keep the beads in a position where they seem to float?" He was talking about my Three Crosses Necklace (pictured on the previous page). At first, I had no idea how to explain it, because I had never analyzed the piece's structure, but after a while I told him, "Maybe it's like the arrangement of stones in the arches of ancient portals. One bead supports the next. If you remove one, everything will collapse."

As a huge enthusiast of RAW—especially because of the many possible ways it can be constructed and embellished—I started a whole series of patterns based on this stitch, and the list continues to grow. It all started with a bracelet made with a RAW base, using 3-mm fire-polished beads, which I then embellished with a beaded version of cross-stitches. I thought about ways of making the design more dimensional, so I built different bases of cubic RAW that were embellished in second and third steps. Those first projects, Tweed Bracelet and Baroque Dimensional Bracelet (at right), have a longitudinal rope of cubic RAW, so they're stiff, like bangles. To create a more flexible version, I created RAW Ribs Bracelet and, later, Centipede Bracelet and Cubic Dots Bracelet (next page).

The middle line of beading in Baroque Dimensional Bracelet, which is related to the horizontal line of beading in RAW Ribs Bracelet, gives the entire piece its shape and curve due to the size of the 3-mm pearls. You'll understand this when you bead step 5 of RAW Ribs Bracelet. This one step determines the shape.

Raw Ribs Bracelet

Tweed Bracelet

Baroque Dimensional Bracelet

Centipede Bracelet

What do all these designs have in common? The basic structures and techniques are identical: a base of elements made from 4-mm fire-polished beads in cubic RAW, a layer of embellishments above the squares of the lattice, and—and this is the most important thing—one last layer that not only covers the crossing points of thread with beads but also gives the piece its final shape by using different sizes of beads.

Once you have the knowledge of a basic stitch under your belt, you can experiment with orientation, bead size, bead count, and thread path. You don't have to follow the fundamental pattern anymore. I constantly experiment with RAW, and that's what I encourage you to do. Create your own bases, and try out the multitude of possibilities. A simple switch from a horizontal to a vertical direction, for example, changes the flexibility of the beadwork completely. The size of the beads added in the last step determines the shape of the piece. Test various diameters; it sometimes requires several tries to find the perfect choice.

Cubic Dots Bracelet

There are many ways to alter bases or embellishments to create different kinds of necklaces, bracelets, beaded beads, and beyond. Another versatile technique is to cover sets of larger beads with netting; doing so lends not only strength but also rich embellishment. Here, too, I've worked in RAW, but due to the different bead sizes, it's no longer easy to identify the single RAW unit. I'm not sure where this design journey specifically started, but Alhambra Bracelet (below) was the first in this series. It consists of a row of RAW units made from pearls of different sizes, covered and surrounded with netting made of smaller beads, and highlighted with crystals to embellish larger areas.

After making Alhambra Bracelet, I wanted to break free from the straight line of its geometry and instead create a curved version by using different bead sizes on the left and the right sides. While finish-ing the first three units, I dropped the idea of a curved bracelet altogether and continued beading until I had a ring shape that required closing. This design was still too limp to become a piece of jewelry, so I added a rivoli in the middle … and Granada Brooch was born. This is a typical example of how I create my beadwork. I start with a certain idea and midway through, it turns into something completely different. Writing these words reminds me that the curved version of Alhambra Bracelet is still on my to-do list!

Let It Grow Bracelet (next page) was also designed as a result of this stepping-stone method. The leaves between the blos-soms are made using the same technique as in Alhambra Bracelet. The bezeled com-ponents use the same kind of arcs, but by pulling them to the middle, they end up filling a completely different function. They become part of a dimensional form: the blossom!

Creating pieces like the ones shown here requires a large variety of bead sizes and bead shapes. It's not terribly important to own an endless number of colors (in the end, we all have our favorite shades) but having lots of shapes and sizes on hand is essential. If you need a bead for the center of two crossing lines of beads, you might choose a size 11°. But if instead you were to use a drop bead, which requires the same space for the thread path, you'd have a much more impressive bead on top.

Building a RAW lattice from bicones results in small gaps between the beads, because they fit perfectly into the right angles. If you use fire-polished beads, however, the lattice becomes smoother, with larger gaps between the beads. Sometimes students ask me if a fire-polished bead is merely a cheaper equivalent to a bicone. No, it is not! It's a completely different shape!

Granada Brooch

Alhambra Bracelet

Again take a look at the vertical middle line of RAW Ribs (page 28, step 5). A 3-mm round bead is added in the center. You could use a bicone here instead, but it wouldn't cover the area in the same perfect way. In fact, if you used too high a thread tension in the basic structure, maybe a round wouldn't even fit. (If you were then to use a drop bead instead, the problem would be easily solved.)

I used a completely different thought process to design the Renaissance Bracelet (below). Influenced by the movie *Romeo and Juliet*, with its beautiful costumes and those very special slashed sleeves that allow a glimpse of the fabric beneath, I began beading with a very specific idea in mind. I wanted to create a bracelet with large pearls in the base that would be visible between the rich embellished surface. My first trial with cylinder beads was a failure because the beadwork was too stiff and the pearls didn't show. Further attempts continued not to work because although I increased the distance between the top layers, the pearls remained hidden. It required a special star-shaped construction around the pearls to open up the gap in the beadwork and make those pearls visible.

When I'm asked about how I make color choices for my jewelry, my immediate response is, "I open my drawers and pick out what I like." This isn't really a proper, well-thought-out answer, but most of the time I do choose colors intuitively.

Color is a question of your own likes and dislikes. There's only a very small number of shades that I don't use; I'm receptive to most colors. There are, however, two major rules that I keep in mind:

Every color has its own gray scale. If you bead with two colors that have identical gray scales, even if they seem to be completely different—like red and green, for example—there will actually be no contrast between the two shades. You can check the gray scale of any hue by taking a digital photo of it and converting it to a black-and-white picture on your computer. This is an especially important aspect to consider when you want to showcase a section of your beadwork. If you're in any doubt, take a picture of the selected beads with your digital camera and check the gray scale. You will be surprised!

Renaissance Bracelet

Let It Grow Bracelet

The same effect takes place when you choose too many different beads with shiny or metallic effects. Two metallic colors placed adjacent to each other show no contrast. On the other hand, a sparkling crystal next to a matte bead shines beautifully.

The pictures on this page show the effect of gray scales on samples of my Hexagonal Twinklestuff Bracelet. In the example at right, before being stitched up, the red-brown beads shimmered with a rainbow effect and the dark brown with a metallic effect, and the colors seemed quite dissimilar. The gray scale, however, shows almost no distinguishable difference. As you can see, the contrast between the bead colors isn't strong enough to show the pattern well. Make sure that the contrast is strong enough by checking the gray scale using the picture test with a small mix of the beads you plan to use, or bead a little test piece. You'll avoid disappointments later on.

Another trick that makes a piece really eye-catching can be gleaned from a color wheel. When making a piece that's tone on tone, you can add a little spot of color from the other side of the color wheel to create very special effects. Examples of opposing colors (called complementary colors) are green and red, yellow and purple, and blue and orange. Note how

Hexagonal Twinklestuff Bracelet

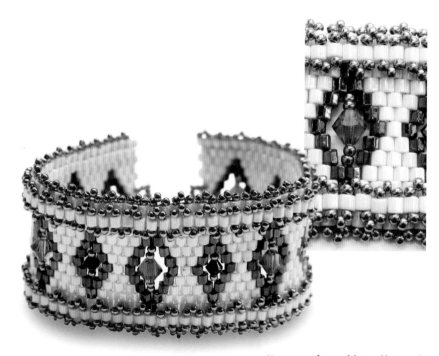

Hexagonal Twinklestuff Bracelet

the turquoise and copper beads play off of each other in this version of Baroque Dimensional Bracelet (at right) and how I've added a little red spot in a green free-form bracelet representing underwater vegetation (at right).

The crochet rope below has a basic pattern of blue and green stripes, with red floral designs. Here, the contrast is increased by choosing shiny beads for the stripes and matte beads for the flowers. Just try out this technique, choosing your favorite shade and mixing it with little spots of color from the opposite side of the color wheel. You'll enjoy the interesting effects.

There are so many things to consider when creating a piece of beadwork. While many things happen intentionally, others happen by trial and error and happy accident. Each bead you string will propel you on this journey, and with time comes experience. I hope this section gave you useful insight into my way of creating and beading, and that it will encourage you to bead in your own unique way!

Baroque Dimensional Bracelet

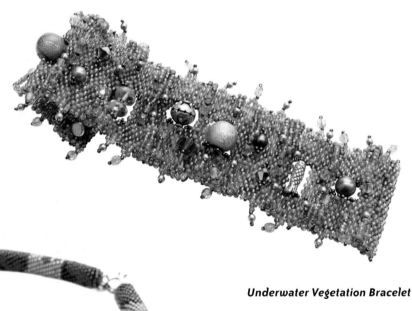

Underwater Vegetation Bracelet

Crochet Rope

TOP

FLORENCE TURNOUR

Metallic Octahedral Cluster Necklace, 2005

40 x 2 x 2 cm

Seed beads; lace overlay

PHOTOS BY GWEN FISHER

LEFT

SHERRY SERAFINI

Chimney Sweeper's Daughter, 2011

43.2 x 19.1 cm

Seed beads, brushes, chain;
bead embroidery, peyote stitch

PHOTOS BY ARTIST

TOP

MARCIA DECOSTER

Lilliana, **2011**

3.8 x 11.4 cm

Beads; right angle weave

PHOTO BY ARTIST

CENTER

EVELYN PUERSCHEL

Bubbles, **2009**

9 x 20 cm

Czech glass beads, vintage nail heads, vintage crystal chatons, freshwater pearls

PHOTO BY SVENJA BOEHME

BOTTOM

EVELYN PUERSCHEL

Blubb, **2008**

5 x 20 cm

Vintage Czech glass cabochons, vintage Arthür Freirich clasp

PHOTO BY SVENJA BOEHME

VEZSUZSI

Bartal, **2011**

6 x 2.5 x 2.5 cm

Gemstone beads, seed beads; RAW

PHOTO BY BUDAI SZILVIA

VEZSUZSI

Vlad, **2011**

5 x 3 x 3 cm

Seed beads; peyote stitch

PHOTO BY BUDAI SZILVIA

133

SABINE LIPPERT'S BEADED FANTASIES

TOP LEFT

GWEN FISHER

Infinity Donut in Blue and Lime, 2008

3.1 x 1.6 cm

Seed beads; infinity weave

PHOTO BY ARTIST

TOP RIGHT

GWEN FISHER

*Seven Sisters Beaded Pendant in Orange
and Purple,* 2008

3.3 x 3.3 x 1.4 cm

Glass beads, cubic zirconia, carnelian,
seed beads

PHOTO BY ARTIST

BOTTOM

GWEN FISHER

Textile Cuff Bracelets VI—Cool Waters, 2009

21 x 8.5 x 0.5 cm

Wool, silk, sparkle fiber, thread, seed beads,
snaps; wet felted, bead embroidery

PHOTO BY ARTIST

SHERRY SERAFINI

Carnival of Artists, 2010

35.6 x 17.8 cm

Seed beads, Czech beads, crystal; bead embroidery, peyote stitch

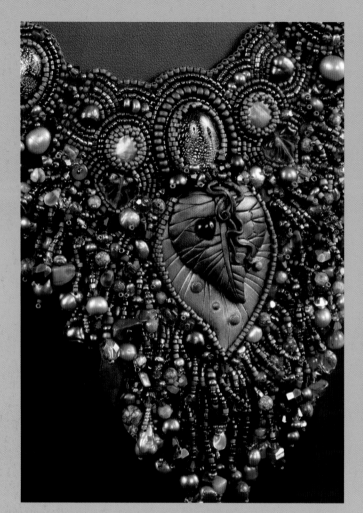

TOP

NANCY DALE

Dryad, **2009–2010**

Seed beads, semiprecious stones, polymer clay cabochons and beads; bead embroidery, RAW, fringing

PHOTOS BY SHERWOOD LAKE PHOTOGRAPHY

BOTTOM

NANCY DALE

Regal Cuff and Earrings, **2010**

Cuff, 1.9 x 20.3 cm; earrings, 1.3 x 1.3 cm

Seed beads, chatons, crystals, 14-karat gold-filled ear wires; layered RAW, herringbone stitch

PHOTO BY SHERWOOD LAKE PHOTOGRAPHY

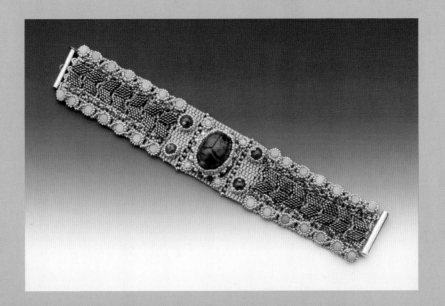

TOP

MAGGIE MEISTER

Olbia Treasure Bracelet, 2010

Cylinder beads, seed beads, ruby scarab, amazonite; RAW, peyote stitch

PHOTO BY GEORGE POST

BOTTOM

MAGGIE MEISTER

Castellani Necklace, 2009

25.4 x 26.7 x 1.3 cm

Assorted cylinder beads, carved soapstone scarabs, 24-karat gold round beads; square stitch, circular brick stitch, brick stitch, backstitch, circular and flat peyote stitch

PHOTO BY GEORGE POST

TOP

Palisades Bracelet, 2011

Seed beads, cube beads, crystals; peyote stitch

PHOTO BY AUTHOR

CENTER

Starball Pendant, 2010

Chatons, seed beads; peyote stitch

PHOTO BY AUTHOR

BOTTOM

Flotsam Necklace, 2010

Raku cabochon by Marianne Kasparian, crystals, pearls, seed beads, brass chain; bead embroidery

PHOTO BY AUTHOR

TOP

Caterpillar Bracelet, 2010

Seed beads, fire-polished beads, crystals, pearls, drop beads; RAW, netting

PHOTO BY AUTHOR

CENTER

Fly Me to the Moon Finger Ring, 2011

Dichroic cabochon by Linda Roberts, seed beads, crystals, metal beads and pendants; bead embroidery

PHOTO BY AUTHOR

BOTTOM

Queen of Spades Bracelet, 2011

Seed beads, glass beads, pearls; bead weaving, RAW

PHOTO BY AUTHOR

TOP

Carnival Bubbles, 2009

Polymer clay beads by DDee Wilder, seed beads, silver-plated chain; peyote stitch

PHOTO BY AUTHOR

BOTTOM

Harlequin Fringes Bracelet, 2009

Seed beads, cube beads, crystals, pearls; peyote stitch

PHOTO BY AUTHOR

TOP

The Dome Pendant, 2010

Seed beads, crystals, glass beads, drop-shaped pearls, rivoli; netting

PHOTO BY AUTHOR

CENTER

Sliders on the Worm, 2010

Seed beads, rivolis, crystals; bead crochet, peyote stitch, netting

PHOTO BY AUTHOR

BOTTOM

Bracelet from the *Sparkle My Wrist* **series,** 2010

Seed beads, crystals, chaton; bead crochet, peyote stitch, RAW, netting

PHOTO BY AUTHOR

ABOUT THE AUTHOR

Born in Germany in the spring of 1967, right on the cusp of the Summer of Love, Sabine Lippert is certain she was destined to one day become a beader. As the daughter of a father who was an engineer and a mother who is a talented painter, she grew up between wits and arts—both of which are so very important for beadwork, in which technique meets beauty. There was no time in Sabine's life when she wasn't crafting, crocheting, tatting, painting, sewing, knitting, or something else of the kind, in search of the perfect material and technique for herself. Being creative has always been an important part of her life, although she chose a rather sensible profession as a physician.

Some years ago, Sabine took her first steps with beads, but due to a lack of good sources, she put them down again. And then one day, in her hometown of Bonn, she came across a bead shop that sold high-quality beads. This changed her life completely. Now Sabine beads before work and continues after returning home, fascinated by the colors, the sparkle, the shapes, and the endless possibilities.

After creating her first patterns, she was asked to teach classes; this was followed by publication in German magazines, and in 2009, her first book, *Das Perlenkochbuch (The Bead Cookbook)*. Although Sabine doesn't specialize in a certain beading technique, there are some that she prefers over others. The skills she gained by doing other forms of crafting help her now in the world of beadwork.

Sabine is a Swarovski Ambassador. She has an online shop at www.trytobead.com; you can see many more examples of her work on her blog, http://try-to-be-better.blogspot.com.

Photo by Dagmar Pappert

ACKNOWLEDGMENTS

To my mother, who gave me creativity, and who with all her love endures the preoccupations of a person deep in the creative process.

To my father, who gave me his technical talent and who will always be a part of me, although he passed away many years ago.

To my family and friends, who understand that I always come around with my beads in tow.

Special thanks to Petra Tismer, whose passion for beads was contagious. She gave me my first seed beads and my earliest opportunities to teach.

To Ray Hemachandra and Nathalie Mornu at Lark Jewelry & Beading, who supported me in every possible way and always had an answer, no matter how strange the question.

Thanks to Judith Durant, who did a brilliant job of technical editing—you're an analytical genius!

To J'aime Allene, for the great illustrations.

And last but not least, to my friend, Verena Greene Christ, who is a master at connecting people; without you, I'm not sure there would be a book at all.

Thanks to all the beaders in the world and to the whole beading community. It's great to be part of this family.

INDEX

INDEX OF CONTRIBUTORS

THE ESSENTIAL LIBRARY OF BOOKS FOR BEADERS

Diane Fitzgerald's
SHAPED BEADWORK

dimensional jewelry
with peyote stitch

Diane Fitzgerald

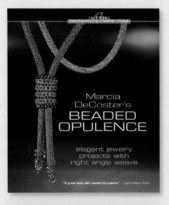

Marcia
DeCoster's
BEADED OPULENCE

elegant jewelry
projects with
right angle weave

Marcia DeCoster

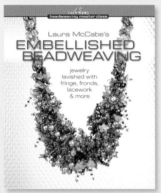

Laura McCabe's
EMBELLISHED BEADWEAVING

jewelry
lavished with
fringe, fronds,
lacework
& more

Laura McCabe

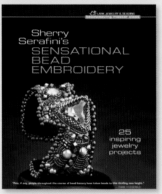

Sherry
Serafini's
SENSATIONAL BEAD EMBROIDERY

25
inspiring
jewelry
projects

Sherry Serafini

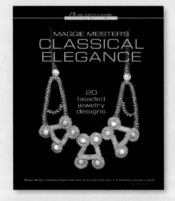

MAGGIE MEISTER'S
CLASSICAL ELEGANCE

20
beaded
jewelry
designs

Maggie Meister

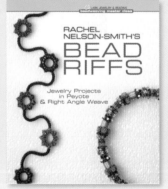

RACHEL
NELSON-SMITH'S
BEAD RIFFS

Jewelry Projects
in Peyote
& Right Angle Weave

Rachel Nelson-Smith

JAPANESE BEADWORK WITH
SONOKO NOZUE

26
Jewelry Designs
from a
Master Artist

Sonoko Nozue

SABINE LIPPERT'S
BEADED FANTASIES

30 Romantic
Jewelry Projects

Sabine Lippert